A Life Among the Dead

A Life
Among
the
Dead

Stories from an Irish Funeral Director

David McGowan

HEADLINE

For Aileen, Mary, Bríd and Eithne

First published in 2024 by
HEADLINE PUBLISHING GROUP

2

Cataloguing in Publication Data is available from the British Library.

Hardback ISBN: 978 1 0354 1222 8
Trade paperback ISBN: 978 1 0354 1223 5

Designed and typeset by EM&EN
Printed and bound in Great Britain by Clays Ltd, Elcograf S.p.A.

MIX
Paper | Supporting
responsible forestry
FSC® C104740

HEADLINE PUBLISHING GROUP
An Hachette UK Company
Carmelite House
50 Victoria Embankment
London EC4Y 0DZ

www.headline.co.uk
www.hachette.co.uk

Contents

Foreword: How We Say Goodbye

THE ONE THING that we can know for certain in this life is that one day we will leave it, and we will lose people who we care about deeply. It's often said that grief is the price we pay for love, and I think there is a lot of truth in that. And yet, despite the inescapable fact that it comes to us all, for so many of us, death seems to be one of the hardest topics in the world to talk about.

But sometimes we have to. As a funeral director, it's my job to guide the bereaved through the process of what happens, from when they suffer their loss to when their loved one is placed in the ground or cremated, and often beyond. I sometimes find myself offering support to people who need it in the weeks, months or even years after their loss. I can't take away the pain of grief, but I see it as my calling to help the grieving through this stage of their journey, to look after the practicalities and allow them a chance to say goodbye.

Perhaps we don't talk about death because we are wary of attracting it. Maybe we are superstitious and don't want to even name it. Or, more likely, the thought of our own mortality is too overwhelming. Perhaps our worst fear is losing a loved one and we cannot bring ourselves to think about such a terrible thing happening. These are very natural and understandable reactions, but I still believe that we need to talk about death. Because the more something is avoided, the more we hide away from it, the harder it will be to cope with when it does eventually visit. And having lived and worked among the dead for nearly fifty years, I don't believe it needs to be this way.

In Ireland, and particularly in the West of Ireland, where I grew up, where I set up my first funeral home thirty-five years ago and where I still live and work, we have strong traditions around what we do when someone dies. Some of these rituals have been adapted a little to fit with our modern ways of living, but many endure intact, having been passed down the generations. When someone dies where I am from, we put ourselves out to help the bereaved get through the funeral, even if it means taking time off work to be there for a friend.

When I was studying death care as a younger man, the Irish wake was something of intrigue to those outside of the tradition (though it was also sometimes presented simply as an excuse for lots of drinking). But in more recent years, I have noticed that there is more understanding of and respect for our traditions, even to the point where I have heard the question asked, 'Why do the Irish grieve better than anyone else?'

Now, I don't know if that is true or not. But I do know that when someone dies here, the community comes together to show great support for the family of the deceased. People will always hear when someone has passed away and often line the streets as the hearse goes by to show their respect. It's not unusual for thousands to turn out for a funeral. We like to celebrate the life of the person we have lost, as we mourn them.

Wakes don't always go on all night anymore, with someone always sitting with the body. But it is still the norm to visit with the deceased, to see them and to say a final goodbye, whether that is in their home or in the funeral home.

That is where embalming, another vital part of my job, comes in. I believe it is everyone's right to see their loved one to say goodbye if they want to, and I have seen time and time again how this can bring comfort. I have explained the practical side of what I do, how I look after someone after they have died, in a chapter titled 'The Science of Death'. I understand that though I am asked about this side of my work often, not everyone will want to know the details, particularly, perhaps, if they have just suffered a loss themselves. So I have gathered this information in one chapter so it can be skipped over if that is what feels right. The same goes for the chapter on the tragic and sudden deaths

I have been called out to in the course of my career titled 'Recovering the Dead'.

Another question I am asked often is how I came to be a funeral director and what it is like to work with the deceased. It is certainly a vocation, and I see why those who do not feel it might struggle to understand. People are often surprised when I explain that for some time when I was first married, my wife and I lived above the funeral home with our small girls, and they played around the place when there were no mourners visiting. So I have begun this book by telling the story of how my father bought a pub and a shop in the village of Easkey in the 1970s that happened to come with a hearse. And I have also shared the story of how I decided to move from rural Ireland to Chicago – a city that saw about eight murders per week and couldn't have been more different to where I was from – in the 1980s to study mortuary science.

None of us can know exactly what happens to us after death. We all have different views. For some of us, these views might be informed by our faith. I cannot believe that when we die, it is just like a light going out and we are no more. I often feel a spiritual presence when I work with the deceased, and I believe that I help their spirit to part with the body that represented them in life. I have experienced so many hard-to-account-for things in the course of my work that go well beyond coincidence.

Death creates an unimaginable void in the lives of the living. Grief is a terribly painful and mixed emotional process. It is a difficult journey that begins with the departure of a loved one, in whatever way that comes. Sometimes death knocks quickly, giving no notice, and other times it pulls and drags in the most painful way, over a long period of time. Death can leave behind its horrific wrath, rendering a deceased person unrecognisable to the living. I feel that my calling is to help connect the living with happy memories of their loved one. I do this by using the skills taught to me, but also those skills that come naturally to me in my work.

It takes a certain type of person to be a good funeral director, just as it takes a combination of skills, knowledge and care to be a good embalmer. In these pages, I want more than anything to demystify what happens when a loved one who has passed is entrusted to my care. I hope that this will give solace to anyone who has lost someone and will be of comfort when such a sad event happens in the future. I want to encourage people to talk openly about death, so that we will better be able to comfort each other in times of grief, express our wishes to our loved ones around our own passing and even feel just a little more prepared for that inevitable day.

The Village of Easkey

EASKEY, COUNTY SLIGO, in the 1960s and early 1970s was not unlike any other rural village in Ireland at the time. Days were punctuated by the sound of the Angelus bell from the local church, and of children playing in the local school. We loved to play football in the school yard with coats or jumpers serving to mark the spot where the goals were. Another favourite pastime of ours was playing a game called handball up against the gable of the school.

A donkey and cart was a must for any farmer for transporting barrels of water and hay. When I stayed at my father's employee P. J. Sloyan's house in Rathlee during the holidays, it was fun to tackle the donkey and cart to bring water to the animals in the fields down the road. The added bonus I quickly cottoned onto was that any American tourists in the vicinity loved the sight of a donkey, and would give me money if I let them take a photo. P. J. often wondered why it always took me so long to return from the fields. When he realised, he used to joke about me, saying, 'That fella will never go hungry.' The donkey cart, though slow, was also a great way to get to and from the bog peatland to save the turf (dried peat) which would be burned as fuel in the wintertime.

Our postman was Martin Connolly. When he finished his deliveries, he set to work as the village blacksmith. I loved to go there to watch him shoe the horses for the local farmers. It was great fun the odd time we got the job of riding the newly shod horse back to its owner.

A morning, midday and evening bus passed through the villages on the roads between the bigger towns. I got the bus each day once I started at secondary school in Enniscrone, a few miles away. It was great to catch up with friends on the short journey. Until then, I'd generally walked home most days from the primary school in Quigabar, which was close to my home, in the company of my siblings and my school friends. We often enjoyed this free time. We loved to pick blackberries when they were in season, and knew to avoid the ones that had a dark centre – an indication of them having gone bad – when you picked them.

Only a small number of households in each parish had cars, though lifts would be generously offered to neighbours for longer journeys when the need arose. Many villages had someone who operated an informal taxi service in their private car. Every house had a 'high Nelly', which was a large black bicycle with the high bar for men and no bar for women. This was the most common mode of transport. A busy day in town would be clearly evident from the bicycles parked up outside the shops.

In those days, teachers educated rigidly in schools, with rote learning at the fore. They had very few resources. The first thing that greeted you on entry to the school was a crucifix, with blood flowing from Jesus's hands. It was a daunting sight to meet every morning. Looking at that cross, we were reminded that that man had died for us, which was a difficult concept for a child to understand. Every senior classroom had a blackboard, globe, a map of the world, and maps of Ireland, both physical and political. Most important was a copy of the Proclamation of the Irish Republic of 1916. This was a large document of poster size that was issued to all schools, marking the foundation of the Irish free state and listing the signatories of the 1916 Easter Rising.

A curriculum guided completely by slaving through textbooks page by page was followed rigidly by our teachers. Oddly enough, there didn't seem to be any purpose to some of the things we laboured over for hours on end. I recall being hit with the edge of a ruler by my first teacher. If a child didn't have their homework done to her satisfaction, she would make them stand at the blackboard and say 'I am a dunce' to the whole class. There were only two classrooms in that school, so when I got to the age of progressing to the senior room, I was delighted. Unfortunately, things weren't a lot better there, with the ruler being replaced by a leather strap known as a 'black jack' for any misdemeanours. We couldn't wait to get out the door at three o'clock to escape the torture in that building.

Until the 1980s, corporal punishment was the normal way to keep children in order, and today we know that it took its toll in the long term. It is hardly surprising that most children didn't object to a day picking potatoes or saving turf instead of going to school, when the opportunity arose. A day's work at home was a lot harder than a day in school but, in many cases, it was less stressful.

Life in general was at a different pace back then, and was very in tune with the environment. People worked with the rhythm of nature, with patience and wisdom. Easkey is on the north-west coast. The Atlantic Ocean was a beautiful sight in calm weather, and the sunsets were the best you could witness, but storms coming in from the Atlantic were severe. Everyone battened down for a storm and waited for it to be over. Life paused at times like this, and it was no big deal. People had a chance to chat and reminisce. It was a life full of mindfulness at its best, at a time when we had never heard of 'mindfulness' or 'wellbeing'.

Families in general all knuckled down to get seasonal jobs done. There was no question of payment for chores like growing vegetables, saving hay or going to the bog to save turf. It was also normal for young people to help for free with whatever it was that their parents worked at to earn a living. This was how our house operated too.

I had three brothers and four sisters, so it was quite a busy house with all of us. My father ran a thriving business selling fertiliser and other products to farmers. He also bought their farm produce – pigs, potatoes, wrack and seaweed from the shore – which he in turn sold on. My older brother and I were regularly called on to help in the yard. We worked hard and there was little point in complaining about blisters or cuts. We just got on with it. I lifted bags of coal and fertiliser from my early teens onwards.

School was not a priority in my father's busy working life. Toys and books were something my mother would raise funds for, from my father or her own father. She loves Irish culture and used to bring us to Irish dancing lessons and *feiseanna* (Irish dancing competitions) when we were younger. We kids used to gather glass bottles and return them to shops to collect the refund on them. This was our main source of income for sweets at the time – unless a generous auntie or uncle came visiting and gave us money for sweets.

It was a priority to 'feed the working men', and the working day revolved around mealtimes, on the farms and in my father's yard. It was difficult for my mother raising eight children while having to make food for all the men who worked in my father's business. One regular favourite dish of hers was cally, which is mashed potatoes with spring onions. I loved to make a hole in the centre of my cally and pour milk in to mix with the potato as I ate it. That was yummy!

We lived in a male-dominated society. A marriage bar forcing women to leave their jobs in the civil service when they got married had been brought in by the government in the 1920s, as a cost-saving initiative, and this practice became widespread in most workplaces. This bar was lifted in 1973. It showed how women were thought to belong in the home – though, of course, their domestic work was often taken for granted.

Until the lifting of that bar, men were the breadwinners in the household, and many controlled the purse strings. They were usually happy, however, to leave any decisions that didn't interest them to the women. Women had to do a lot of *plámásing* (empty flattery) of their husbands to be allowed to purchase the items their husbands might consider a luxury.

My father liked to keep a close account of finances in our house. Though he often celebrated the conclusion of a successful period of work in the local pub, which was a good time to ask him for extra money.

For the most part, Irish society followed the unwritten societal rules. You worked all week and went to Mass on Sunday. Missing Mass was a big thing, and if you failed to attend, there would be speculation. It was unheard of to work on a Sunday unless you had a really good excuse (though publicans were exempt from that rule). Many of those who disagreed with these rules and conventions found it easier to emigrate and enjoy the freedom afforded to them in America, Australia, England and other countries, where they could be among people of different belief systems. For many, another draw was the luxury of being anonymous, having come from small communities where everyone needed to know too much about each other.

The Christian churches, mostly Catholic, had a strong grip on the people, who followed the doctrine of the Church to the letter of the law. Irish people had great faith, and the local priest was usually the first to be consulted on any matters arising in the parish. His decision would often lead the way. It was normal for this strong Christian society to dress up in their best clothes for Sunday worship. The 1917 Code of Canon Law required women to cover their heads and dress modestly when attending religious ceremonies or visiting a church. It was usual for women to wear a head veil called a mantilla to Mass, in keeping with this rule. The rule was eased in the late 1970s and disappeared in 1983. Men were required to remove their caps at worship during this period.

Families usually sat down to a Sunday roast after church, and this was often followed by everyone heading to a local football match, with some ending up in a pub on the way home. I guess the rule about Sunday being a day of rest didn't include the work women did in the kitchen in preparing the Sunday dinner! My mother, like other women, often went to the early Mass and got to work in the kitchen afterwards, while my father tended to go to the later Mass. More often than not, we went with my mother. We loved her Sunday roast chicken or beef. Some Sundays, my father would go away in the car, buying pigs from farmers. There were no weighing scales, so the weight was always estimated.

Gaelic football has always been the revered game in the West of Ireland. Each parish had a football team, though our pitches were not carefully groomed fields with dressing rooms and lights. I played underage football with the Easkey Sea Blues throughout my teenage years. Teams had to come from inside the parish boundary. This was a rule usually strictly adhered to, though we lived on the borderline of two parishes, so we escaped it. On one occasion, I played with Easkey against my brother's team in the neighbouring parish. Easkey pitch was great to play on on a calm day, but quite the opposite when the harsh Atlantic wind was against you in the final minutes of a game. As beautiful white, foamy Atlantic waves crashed on the dark limestone rocks nearby, there was no shelter from the winds on the pitch, which had a huge impact on any game there. Any perceived injustices, or things unnoticed by the referee during the game, were often sorted off-pitch afterwards, and Easkey was well known for its victories!

Most villages had a few shops, and Easkey was a thriving place in that respect. The one main street had four small grocery shops, a chemist, a hairdresser, a petrol pump and a clothes shop, not to mention four more pubs. The post office in Easkey also had a grocery shop at the front. To the rear of the shop was the post office counter, along with the telephone exchange, where an operator connected calls to the few people in the parish who had a phone. Phone calls were connected by village name and then to the individual number concerned. You might even catch a faint fragment of a phone conversation if you happened to be within earshot of the exchange and everything was silent around you. The system was basic but it sufficed. This meant that in the mid-to-late 1970s, we didn't normally get called about a death. Those who had a phone usually didn't pay the extra charge to avail of a night service between 10pm and 8am, which meant a number of houses sharing the same line at night time. Each household had to listen each time the phone rang to ascertain if the number of rings matched the number for their house. Of course, those curious about calls received in other houses might 'accidentally' lift the phone and overhear a conversation. Phone calls were expensive, and people who had phones watched the clock carefully when they made a phone call.

The local grocery shops stocked essential items, such as bread, flour, sugar, tea, biscuits, canned fruit and vegetables, gas and some general items. There wasn't a wide range of products. Most farming households had their own eggs, fresh vegetables, butter, milk and bacon. Most households had their own vegetable plots. People rarely bought potatoes in a shop and most had their own supply of onions, carrots, parsnips, peas and cabbage.

Shops generally allowed customers credit, as people often got paid at the end of each month. Some shops kept a large ledger for this, while others had individual notebooks for each customer. I remember having to fill in details of items bought on credit in our business and keeping copious records of the monthly payments.

Two of the grocery shops had a bar at the back. On entry to the shop, you would be met with a counter on either side. An attendant (usually the owner) served you and placed the goods you had requested on the counter, before totting up the total cost on a notebook. Men who had cycled to town often just handed the attendant the shopping list their wives had given them, then they would go through to the bar at the rear to quench their thirst while the order was being filled. They would pay for and pick up a neatly packed box containing their goods, which fitted on the carrier of the bicycle. There was no plastic waste back then and almost everything was reused, a long time before the term 'recycling' came about!

In 1974, my parents purchased Paddy Browne's business in Easkey, a typical grocer's with the aforementioned counters and a pub attached for the sum of IR£12,500. A pub was a good business to have in Ireland because it was the only social outlet mostly for men. It was said at the time that a foot (in length) of a counter was as good as an acre of land. The pub and grocer's was a thriving business.

I learned of the purchase one morning when I was in the bedroom where I shared a large double bed with my three brothers, as we were in the middle of building an extension to the house at the time. I overheard my father talking to a farmer in the hallway, who had come to pay for fertiliser. In the course of the conversation, my father was asked if it was true that he had bought Browne's business in Easkey. I heard him respond, 'Yes.' I remember being so excited about this new venture. Would we be moving from the countryside to live in the village of Easkey? Believe me, that was as big a move as moving to a city for me! A lot of my friends who I played football with lived in or close to the village. I thought that there would be much less work to do in a pub, and so I wouldn't have to help out so much, and would have great fun playing football instead. Little did I know that it would entail far more work for me.

After my father had agreed the price for the business, he was asked if he wanted to carry on the funeral business associated with the premises. He was told that there was a new hearse that had recently been purchased for IR£1,500, and that he would have to pay this extra cost if he wanted to continue the funeral business. He said that he knew nothing about funerals and wasn't sure if he would continue with this side of things. When he went to do a full survey of the premises, he looked at the hearse and found that it scared him. He wouldn't carry on this business, he decided. So he rang the solicitor to confirm his decision.

However, the solicitor told him to talk to some of the locals who helped with that side of things before making his final decision. Following a few conversations, he realised that he would have enough help. Alfie Morrison was the hearse driver, Johnny Kavanagh mounted (meaning he screwed fixtures around the sides) and lined coffins and looked after graves, and local nurses and other women looked after the laying out of the deceased. My father was told that all he had to do was turn up with a hearse and a coffin. The hearse was a new Opel estate car, with a bubble-shaped back window to accommodate the extra length of a coffin. The car was sometimes jokingly referred to as the pregnant hearse because of this bulbous window. The coffins were stacked in a shed at the back of the pub.

In those days, all the undertaker was really needed for was to provide the coffin, put the deceased in the coffin and to transport the coffin and the deceased. The concept of funeral homes only really existed in the big cities and was practically unheard of where we lived. So it didn't seem a problem that our family knew nothing about funerals! My father decided that he would be happy to show up for the funeral ceremony and let the men who had worked for the previous owner continue as they had done for years.

The Pub with a Hearse

IN IRELAND, we have always had a very special dedication to death and funerals, and the culture that surrounds these things is distinct from those found in other places around the world. Yes, there are commonalities, of course, but in general, we have a particular perspective on death and it is firmly embedded in our culture.

From early megalithic sites to the most modern concept of the columbarium wall – a custom-built wall for keeping urns of the ashes of the deceased – the people of Ireland have always been deeply committed to honouring the dead. While there are many common customs around the country, each area has its own peculiarities. Traditionally, men and women had distinctly different roles in these rites and everyone fell naturally into their parts when required.

If someone died in a hospital, the nurses often fixed up the person in the ward before the body was taken to the mortuary. The hospital porter generally helped put the deceased person into the coffin once they had reached the mortuary. If they had died at home, the local nurse usually came and laid out the person on their bed. Everyone left the room to allow her to do her work, though sometimes the women in the house would help her wash and dress the dead person. The nurse would set the face and position the head and hands of the corpse before rigor mortis set in.

If the nurse wasn't able to be present, it was traditional for a group of women to wash the remains. They kept the water they'd used to be thrown in front of the hearse as a mark of respect for the dead. Once they were finished getting the deceased dressed, they called the men, who would come in and lift the deceased into the coffin. It was all very discreet, private and respectful.

While this was happening, the family and those who knew the person waited for the deceased to be over-board, a term which referred to the person being laid out, or prepared for reposal (where friends and family come to pay their respects ahead of the funeral). Up until about the 1990s, it was the custom for Roman Catholics to be laid out in a habit, a long garment similar to those worn by monks and nuns. The habit for a man was brown with an image of Jesus on the chest, while women were usually dressed in a blue habit with an image of the Blessed Virgin. Young people and children were laid out in white. The habit had to be blessed by the priest before it was used to dress the deceased. If a habit wasn't to be used, the person would be laid out in their own best outfit, often a suit and tie for men and a dressy outfit for women. A window was opened in the room where the person had died so that the person's spirit could leave. After two hours, the window was closed again to ensure that the spirit didn't return to the body and also that other spirits didn't enter the house.

Word would go around once the person was over-board and people would know to begin visiting the wake house. A wake is when the deceased person is kept at home for one or more nights. They are never left alone during this period. One of the Irish words for wake is *faire* which means keeping a vigil, watching over the deceased to protect them from any bad spirits. The wake would last for at least a full night – if the person had died after midnight, the wake wouldn't usually start until the following night. It was un-heard of to leave the deceased alone during the wake.

From the point at which locals got the word that the deceased was over-board until the removal of the deceased to a church, there would be a fairly large gathering of people at the house at all times, with the quietest times being in the middle of the night. The house was open for all who came, and food and drink were plentiful. In older times, clay pipes and tobacco were provided for those attending. Cigarettes were also popular.

A wake has a mix of all emotions. Of course, it is a very sad time for all, especially those closest to the deceased. However, it is also an opportunity to reminisce about the good times. If the deceased had any interest in music, then that will be a part of the wake. Their favourite local musician will almost certainly turn up at some stage to play. Songs are sung, with songs associated with the deceased or similar circumstances evoking an emotional wave of sadness among the grieving. The wake is usually interspersed with prayers for the deceased and other deceased persons related to them. Candles are always burned near the coffin in the wake house or in the funeral home. For many, a lit candle serves as a way to honour the person, paying tribute in some way to the life they have lived. It also symbolises the continuation of the life of the deceased in spirit. I can remember keeners coming to a wake, crying, and wailing for hours on end. The Irish word for cry is *caoin*, and I suspect this is where the word 'keeners' came from. This is a tradition that died out at some time in the 1970s, and was in stark contrast with the farewell parties that often followed. Songs, music and stories continue throughout the night.

Items were placed in the coffin with the person for their journey to heaven. Sometimes even a little bottle of whiskey or poitín (a locally produced spirit) was added for comfort. In farming communities, it wasn't unusual to place a fistful of clay from their land in the coffin to continue their connection with that place as they moved in to the spiritual world. A rosary blessed by the priest was draped around the hands of deceased Catholics, and holy water was always included, in a little bottle purchased in Knock,

Lourdes, Fatima, Medjugorje or other places of pilgrimage. These were to protect the deceased from harm and ensure their safe journey 'home' to heaven.

Catholics believe in a place/state called purgatory, where souls of the deceased go prior to heaven to be purified and cleansed of their sins. It is the belief that living souls can help them through this process through their prayers. Lots of Catholics would wear a scapular around the neck (some still do), as it was believed to protect the wearer from the fires of hell, as promised by the The Blessed Virgin of Mount Carmel (the title given to the Virgin Mary in her role as patroness of the Carmelite Order). The wearing of a scapular was also thought to shorten the deceased's stay in purgatory if they had left this life with a debt of punishment for sins committed. A scapular consisted of two rectangular pieces of felt fabric, approximately three centimetres by two centimetres, each made of two pieces sewn together, with holy pictures and prayers sewn on to the rectangles. Sometimes there was a prayer or relic contained within the pieces, which were joined by two lengths of cord. The whole scapular resembled a necklace that could be worn under clothing. Different colours of scapular represented different things, but brown, representing Our Lady of Mount Carmel, was a favourite with many.

In the West of Ireland, most people practised a Christian faith. There was a respectful relationship between Catholics and Protestants within the community, and it was not rare to have mixed marriages between the different Christian faiths. On the death of a member of a mixed marriage family, clergy from both churches were welcomed in the wake house to say the prayers from their religious ceremonies. There was a period where it was considered a sin for Catholics to enter a Protestant church, which caused a dilemma for some when it came to funerals. Only the bishop had the power to forgive that sin! Thankfully, this is not the case these days.

But sitting alongside the important religious rituals that everyone knew about and expected, there were also various traditions and superstitions. For example, it was essential to turn mirrors to face the wall or to cover them with a cloth for the duration of the wake. It was believed that this would ward off unwanted spirits, closing off all possible access routes for them to enter the house. Watches often mysteriously stopped upon the death of the wearer, and it was often noted that the clock most used by the person who had passed also stopped at the time of death. If it didn't, it would be stopped by someone in the house. On leaving the house to bring the coffin to the church, it was common to turn chairs upside down. This was a sign to unwanted spirits that they were not welcome in the house, as presumably they would see that there wasn't even a seat for them to sit on if they did somehow enter! Lights were left on until the mourners returned to the house later that evening, to confuse spirits by leading them to believe there were people in the house whose prayers would ward them off.

It was important for Roman Catholic family members to get a Mass card signed by the priest. This was a card, similar in size to a greetings card, with a special line for a priest to sign his name and another line for the name of the deceased, for whom a special Mass would be offered. There was usually a religious picture on the front of the card. The priest was given an offering of money for signing the card. This, again, was to help save the person from the fires of hell, as prayers and Masses shortened their stay in purgatory. Sympathy cards were the alternative for non-Catholics, but Catholics often looked at a sympathy card as having some lesser value as it didn't have a Mass intention signed by a priest.

THIS WAS THE CULTURE that I grew up in, and the backdrop to my family's new line of work. Everyone knew what to do when someone passed. The rites and rituals were handed down through the generations.

Though I say 'everyone knew' – I had never been to a funeral prior to my parents taking over the business in Easkey, as I was considered too young. In our area, children weren't exposed to death in the same way as they are today. They were usually taken to a neighbours' house for the duration of the funeral. Sometimes they were brought to the Mass and burial, but for the most part, they were not brought to see the deceased person at a wake.

The funeral business was the smallest part of my father's expanding businesses. Prior to being sold to my parents, it had only dealt with around twelve to fifteen funerals each year, this being the number of people who died locally and needed the services of a hearse. It would have been difficult to make a living from it as a stand-alone business. Nonetheless, after my father bought the bar and shop, it was included in my family's line of work. And, as I have mentioned, all children and adolescents where I grew up were expected to help out sometimes in the way their parents made a living. So it was only a matter of time before I would have first-hand experience of funerals and undertaking.

A year or so after buying the shop and bar, my father and mother set about renovations. We were very proud to have the first Spar supermarket in Easkey, with modern facilities and a checkout – this was the new style of retail, where customers got to select items from shop shelves and pay a cashier near the door, rather than the traditional counters behind which someone would pack up your shopping for you. We even employed a manager, who brought life to the place when he came. The idea of employing a manager was a whole new concept. The shop became a thriving business.

Easkey was flourishing at this stage, and the addition of a clothing factory brought very valuable employment to the area. This was particularly good for women, giving them their own income and independence. Workers often stopped off in the shops in Easkey each Friday to cash their pay cheques, which in turn led to spending in the local economy.

As I have explained, very few people had telephones at this time, so we did not normally hear about a death via a phone call. Sometimes, we might have heard that someone from the parish had died from someone coming into the bar or the shop, or while at the post office. At other times, a small group of men would enter the bar without any advance warning that they were coming. It would be apparent from their disposition that they had sorrowful business to attend to. The awkward silence would often be broken by me or my father saying, 'Have you got trouble?' Meaning, have you lost someone to death?

The priest would usually have been at the house of the deceased, and would have already arranged the times for going to the church for the funeral ceremonies with the bereaved. The next port of call was the visit to the undertaker.

Making funeral arrangements with the family was fairly straightforward back then. It involved confirming times for the religious ceremony, choosing a coffin, organising a grave, laying out the deceased, and ordering food and drink to the wake house. Very often, different aspects of the funeral were looked after by different people. When all was arranged, they would leave quietly, with others in the bar sympathising with them on their way out.

Once they had left, there was plenty to be done, including sending bread, ham, milk, butter, a stock of alcoholic drinks and minerals (as we call soft drink) out to the wake house. A coffin had to be prepared, the hearse washed and filled with fuel, the grave sorted, a death notice called in to the paper. The post office was usually involved in ringing in the death notice to one of the national Irish newspapers. There were three main papers on sale in our area at the time: *The Irish Times*, the *Irish Independent* and the *Irish Press*. Those who had strong political views and supported Fine Gael and independent politicians would prefer to put the death notice in the *Irish Independent*; those who favoured Fianna Fáil usually asked for the *Irish Press*. Business people, academics and people who liked to remain neutral would opt for *The Irish Times*. Local people would know which paper to buy to read the death notice.

In order to submit the notice, we had to check arrangements for the Mass or service time with the priest or parson, then call the paper's head office and read out the entire thing, spelling any unusual people or place names. This was a nerve-wracking affair, as mistakes made at this stage would cause a lot of headaches, as the costs were high. The staff at the newspapers were very competent and had excellent command of English grammar, so we could always rely on them to ensure the wording of the notice was consistent with others in the obituary column. My father or mother usually looked after the death notices until I was old enough to be trusted to do the job.

I WAS AROUND fifteen when I had my first encounter with death. A funeral call had come in and I was instructed to go down and help our part-time employee Johnny Kavanagh, who was a great character, to lift out the coffin. Six bottles of whiskey were to be put in the coffin to bring them to the house. These were in addition to the ones already ordered, which my father thought would be insufficient, as they were going to an area where there were lots of whiskey drinkers.

When we got to the house, I went into the room where the deceased was now ready to be lifted into the coffin. The two cotton balls stuffed up the nostrils of the deceased were not as crude-looking as the bandage around his face, wrapped from the top of the head to under the chin. I asked my father what it was for, and he said it was to keep the mouth closed. I was baffled as to why a dead person would be opening their mouth. He told me to ask the nurse who had done the laying out.

The deceased then had to be lifted, and I was assigned the feet. The toes were tied together too. My imagination was beginning to run away with me. I awkwardly lifted on the count of three and the man was put into the coffin.

The coffin was on the floor at this stage. Apparently, it

was normal to rest the coffin on two chairs, but in this house they needed the chairs for the wake. I was sent out to the hearse to get the trestles from behind the driver's seat, and we placed the coffin on them under the window. I was then sent out again for the candles and holy water from the glove compartment in the hearse.

At this stage, everyone had been given a cup of whiskey. I was given a small drop in a cup too. I hated the smell of whiskey and looked for a place to get rid of it. My father told me it was unlucky not to accept a drink offered to you in a 'corpse house' but I decided to risk it. The room was fairly dark, so I managed to spill it discreetly in the corner of the room without being noticed.

We left and did not return again until the time came to take the coffin to the church. I thought about the whole experience and realised that I had touched a dead person for the first time in my life and I wasn't fazed by it.

My father didn't get involved in laying out the deceased unless no one else was available. As mentioned, a nurse or group of women would usually take charge of this, but it wasn't unheard of for an undertaker to be involved. But in my father's case, I suppose he found the rawness of death difficult. He wasn't alone in having difficulty and fears around working with the deceased. Many people are clumsy and helpless when it comes to doing anything in terms of the laying out and presentation of someone who has died. But as time went on, I found that I had no problem abandoning my work in the bar, and it was certainly easier getting someone to replace me there than it was to find someone who was willing to pitch in with the funeral side of things. I enjoyed being part of it, however, and quickly grew to love getting stuck in to all the jobs that had to be done behind the scenes. I felt drawn to this work, and wanted to spend more and more time working in this part of the business.

Considering how little my father knew about the funeral business to begin with, it was lucky that we had Johnny Kavanagh working for us. He was a real all-rounder when it came to putting you in your box. He took his time with mounting a coffin with the handles and lining it with side sheets (often satin finishes that decorate the inside of the coffin and stretch out over the edges). He often took long breaks for a cigarette, and told many interesting stories. I often wondered if preparing the coffin was a break from the chats rather than the other way around. He knew everything about funerals in the area and was the caretaker for the local cemetery. He used to dig the graves, too, and he did a great job. There was a roster of other men who would turn up and do one job or another, sometimes sliding down from their barstool to help with lifting a coffin into the hearse.

A part-time employee called Jimmy, who was a bit of a character to say the least, used to shave the men who had passed. I was intrigued when I watched him carefully carry out the task. I wondered how he managed to do it so well. He told me he had a little secret. He would put a potato in the man's mouth so that the face would be fuller and thus easier to shave. He would remove the potato again when he had finished. I never saw him use one but he seemed proud of his technique.

On one occasion when I was helping Johnny, he stopped digging and tapped his spade on the lid of the coffin of the last person who had been laid to rest in that family grave. 'How are ye gettin' on there, oul fella?' he joked, and fondly spoke of the man buried underneath him.

He kept with tradition, and under no circumstances would he open a grave on a Monday. He would dig the grave on a Monday, but only if the sod had been turned on a day before that, as this technically meant the grave had been opened on a different day. In our culture, people were very superstitious. They had certain beliefs that had to be adhered to, or else very bad things could happen. To this day, gravediggers in country areas will not open a grave on a Monday, as they believe that if they do, the grave will be opened again within twelve months. The fairies were often blamed when some misfortune occurred – I guess nowadays we might associate some of these things with the universe or karma.

People feared the call of the banshee, as it was a sure indication that a death was imminent. *Bansí* is an Irish word that translates to fairy woman, and describes a female spirit believed to herald the death of a family member by wailing or crying, usually in the night. It was also believed that deaths came in threes, so if one person died, two more were sure to follow.

In my early days of funeral directing, I made the mistake of collecting all the butts from the burned candles in a wake house, putting them in my pocket to later dispose of them. I was promptly reprimanded and had to give back the expired candles. The person explained to me that expired candles used at a wake had the power to cure swelling in any part of the body. I know that people still believe in this cure to this very day.

There were no digging machines back then for digging graves, so they were dug carefully using spades, shovels and a pick if needed. Neighbours would all take a turn at the work, and a bottle of whiskey was shared among all of the participants as they reminisced about the dead person, or others around them in the graveyard.

Usually, all the coffins used in an area were the same size, so our man would know by looking at the grave if it was the right size, and, quite often, no measuring tape was required. However, caskets from America, those of emigrants being repatriated for burial, brought challenges for grave-diggers, as they were usually much larger than the coffins we were used to.

I remember hearing, on one occasion, about a funeral in another county at the time, for which the deceased was coming in from America. The grave was duly dug to accommodate the large American casket. The undertaker in question travelled to Dublin airport to collect the casket and, to his horror, was presented with an urn! He had to stop at the first telephone kiosk he saw to ring home and send word to the gravedigger to reduce the size of the hole that had been prepared. Cremation was frowned upon by the Irish Catholic Church for a long time, and so was a rarity that we only came across when ashes were returned from the United States or the UK to be interred in Ireland. I remember times when ashes brought in from abroad were put in to a coffin and the coffin weighed down with bags of clay or sand so that those carrying it wouldn't know that it contained ashes and not the corpse. As the years went by, cremation first became acceptable in cities and gradually was accepted in rural Ireland. Nowadays, approximately 20 per cent of deceased persons are cremated. Cremation is becoming more and more popular in modern Ireland.

The clergy, for the most part, were kind and supportive of the bereaved. They came to the wake house and said prayers and also called on the bereaved in the weeks following the funeral. Funeral ceremonies were carried out with a great sense of ritual and respect. Whole communities attended the funeral reception in the church, usually in the evening, and returned for the Mass or service the following morning.

The order of the funeral differed slightly around the

country, but in general, a funeral ritual involved bringing the coffin to the church for a requiem Mass or service, and burial took place after that. In most places, it was preferred to keep the deceased in the church for at least one night between the service and burial, to be in the presence of God.

There were beliefs in relation to weather at the time of a funeral. It was often said that if rain fell on the coffin at any stage of the funeral, it represented new growth and cleansing. Older people would say: 'Happy the corpse the rain falls on.' If there was thunder after a burial, it was believed to be a sign that the spirit of the deceased had made it to heaven.

Employers allowed their staff time off to attend funerals of friends and relations, as it was expected that local people would be there. The rhythm of life was so different, and there was no fuss in the workplace about this practice, as death comes to everyone, and the community unselfishly gave up their time and supported the bereaved.

At that time, it was customary for the bereaved of Christian faith to wear black for a period of time following a funeral. This is a custom that has died out over the years, but many people still wear black for the funeral period. Back in the seventies, Catholics wore black for at least one month until 'month's mind' Mass. This was a Mass that took place within a month of the death. It was all part of the ritual. It was believed that the spirit stayed around for about a month, but everyone knew that the spirit had to be released from this world to heaven. The month's mind Mass is often as big as the funeral Mass, with people seeing it as very important to support the bereaved even after the funeral itself is over and done with. It is still as important to this day.

For Catholics, the month's mind Mass marked the freeing of the spirit. After this point, the bereaved could abandon wearing black. However, some continued to wear black for a year and a day. Queen Victoria actually wore black from the time she was widowed to the time of her death, which, in the late nineteenth and early twentieth centuries, may have influenced some to wear black for longer periods of time.

In reality, meeting someone in mourning clothes was a reminder to treat them with some extra kindness and compassion. It wasn't a bad plan, really, when you think about it. How many people return to work these days following a funeral, and many of their colleagues might not even know that they are trying to come to terms with a grief in their lives as they work in a place where others are unaware of their pain?

Some made decisions not to visit the grave after a death, but for the most part, people usually tended to the grave where their loved one had been buried. It was traditional to hold off on putting up a headstone on a grave for at least a year and one day. The logical reason for this was to let the ground settle after the burial, which takes at least six months. If a headstone already existed on the family grave, an inscription could be added at any time after the funeral.

In those days, people showed great kindness and sympathy towards each other when someone died. Everyone set aside any differences they had and gave wholeheartedly and generously of their time to help. The townland stood still for a day or two, and nobody dared show disrespect by carrying on with non-essential work. Neighbours stepped in to look after any essential farm work to enable the bereaved to focus completely on the funeral.

Meitheal is an Irish word meaning 'working party' – it effectively means everybody coming to give whatever help they can when something has to be done. Different times of the year would trigger a *meitheal* event – for example, saving the hay or turf-cutting. Instead of each person doing their own work in their own field or plot, everyone would come along and the group would work together until everyone's jobs were done. The saying 'many hands make light work' was very apt. There was a rhythm to the work, and these were good times when people chatted as they worked, solving many problems along the way. The days were marked with breaks, when workers would pause to have some sandwiches and tea. The women often made bread, scones and lovely sweet cakes.

The *meitheal* extended to funerals too, with everyone doing his or her share of whatever had to be done. The *meitheal* of neighbours set about cleaning and tidying the house for the wake. Sometimes they would even paint any walls that didn't look well. It was all about dignity and respect around the wake and funeral that was to come. Whether the death was sudden or followed an illness, the thinking was that the bereaved were in no frame of mind to be worrying about home décor. It was nice for them not to have to think about anything like that. Everything was done carefully and respectfully. Grass would be cut and hedges clipped. Of course, if there were farm animals to be tended to, the bereaved would be relieved of all duties to enable them to be free to participate in every part of the funeral. The bereaved were supported emotionally, sometimes bringing out tears of laughter mixed with painful tears of grief. It was essential to feed the family and everyone who came to pay their respects. Everyone in the community brought their offerings. The bereaved were surrounded with an outpouring of love and support.

I remember from my time working in the pub how the men would organise where the *meitheal* would come together for the coming days. It was also noted if someone was dodging their work, and they'd be reminded, in no uncertain terms, that their day would come. Dodging your duty was not accepted within the community. Many would say that you couldn't get the farm work done on your own, and that the *meitheal* was an essential part of life.

I once heard a woman tell the story of the day her father died suddenly back in the 1940s near the Nephin mountain. She was a teenager at the time. The *meitheal* had gone up the mountain to harvest a crop, and her father had stayed home as he wasn't feeling well that day. It was a long trek up the mountain, so when you went up there, you went for the full day.

In the late morning, the man's condition deteriorated rapidly and he died. The woman's mother was in shock and distraught. The teenager desperately needed the help of her neighbours. The only way of contacting them on the mountain was the system that they had of putting a white sheet out on a tree, to indicate to that there was some sort of trouble back at the house. And so the mother asked her daughter to take the white sheet off the bed and put it on the highest branch in the garden in the hopes that someone out on the mountain would notice it and realise that something serious was up. Fortunately, someone did spot the sheet and understood that something was wrong. Some of the *meitheal* returned, having agreed another signal for the rest should they have to return too. The *meitheal* helped that family through what was a very traumatic time for them. The woman said they were so grateful for the support from the community. They had felt helpless in their situation, but all was taken care of when the others arrived.

In the years that followed, the lady took the painful, difficult decision to emigrate to America and start a new life there. Times back then were very tough in rural Ireland. She had to cycle about an hour to Ballina to get a train to Galway, and subsequently catch a bus that took her to Shannon Airport. She said she would never forget the experience of the twenty-two-hour flight, as she was sick from the minute she got on the plane to the minute she got off it. It was also very emotionally painful to be leaving her widowed mother behind.

She was only a year or so in America when a telegram arrived telling her that her mother had been buried that morning. While she got huge support from the Irish community there, she had to grieve the loss of her mother without ever seeing her again. She always regretted that. With such a long journey home, it would never have been possible to delay the funeral until her return, as it was not common practice to keep the deceased for long periods back then. This was common for emigrants, many of whom never got to see their beloved parents again. Support from their communities was essential to them in their grief.

I took community support for granted until I went to America myself. It was there that I realised that the *meitheal*, this concept of the whole community coming together and getting involved when someone dies, is a very Irish thing to do. Of course, I now understand that other communities have different thoughts on death. Some prefer to give the bereaved time to grieve alone, and see bereavement as a time when someone needs privacy. But as you can see, where I am from, community is everything.

Chicago

As TIME WENT BY, I continued to work full-time in the bar, but I still preferred the funeral side of the business. I was also becoming increasingly involved with supporting the families and neighbours of the deceased, as well as helping out more with the laying out.

In Ireland at the time, we didn't know or think too much about the science of death and what happens to someone in the days after they die. I was starting to understand, though, how important it was that when friends and relatives attended the wake, the person they were mourning looked as well as they could, and familiar, as they had in life. And so I began to notice little extra things I could do to improve the look of the deceased as they lay in the coffin. But there was a lot to learn and, for the moment, some of it was out of reach for a local undertaker in the West of Ireland.

I soon learned that the decomposition process took its toll in differing ways. We dreaded a funeral where a family member was travelling home from abroad to attend, as that generally meant a delay. A delay in those days was a big worry, knowing what could potentially go wrong. There were no mortuary fridges in those days in which deceased could be stored. Not even the funerals homes in the larger cities had them, and those hospitals that did have this facility would only have space for four deceased persons, maximum.

One day, when I was in my late teens, I noticed Johnny putting a 'scraw' into a coffin. This was a large sod of turf, usually taken from the surface of the bog, and thus had heather on it. When I asked Johnny why he had put it in there, he winked and told me that it would help keep the smell away. I really had no idea of what he meant by this. Of course, he was talking about the decomposition process in the most basic of ways. For him, this was the way to deal with a problem, and while there may have been something scientific behind it, for the most part it was simply what was done in that situation. At least it gave you the feeling that you had tried to do something, no matter how futile it appeared!

The more experience I gained in those first few years, the more I learned about problems that can occur with the deceased. For the most part, we didn't experience too many issues in the early days, but when they did occur, the consequences were awful for everyone. There was no way of predicting when these issues might arise. But by the late seventies, it felt like more problems were arising that even the nurses couldn't remedy. I don't know if I was just becoming more aware of these problems at this point, or whether it was down to more people dying in hospital, where they would have been increasingly given more medication prior to passing. As far as I am aware, no scientific study has been done into this.

I recall one occasion when we were sent for to solve the issue of an odour coming from the remains as they lay in the wake house. This, of course, was the decomposition process setting in, but there was little we could do about this at the time. My father had no idea what to do when they called him, so he referred them to the local doctor to see if he could help them out. When I think back on it, it's no wonder that the doctor, who was particularly busy at the time, could not come to assist, as his focus had to be on the living.

When we arrived at the house where the deceased was laid out, the only thing my father could suggest was that we put the lid on the coffin and place it outside in the garden for the wake. Fortunately, the weather was mild and everyone accepted this solution. But I remember feeling very embarrassed. I really wished that we knew how to help people when these situations arose.

On another occasion, I remember travelling to a Dublin hospital to collect a deceased person. At that time, a person who died in Dublin would be brought straight from the hospital to the church the day before the funeral, with the immediate family following the hearse from Dublin and other cars joining the cortège closer to the church. I will never forget the smell from the coffin during the five-hour journey from Dublin on that day. I had to lean out of the open passenger window to escape the odour, the whole way from Dublin. It must have been some sight to see a hearse coming with a young fella leaning out the window. There was plenty of incense in the church that evening!

Friday nights were very busy in the village and at the pub, with bingo in the village hall. The busiest time on a Friday night in the bar was when there was a half-hour break in the bingo, as there would be a rush to the pubs for a quick hot whiskey. That was some pressure, trying to get everyone served and back in the hall for the second part of the bingo – after all, the biggest prize on the 'pool sheet', a full house, could be worth £50.

One such Friday, my father travelled to Dublin for a funeral. When a person passed away in a hospital in Dublin, family members and some close friends and neighbours would travel to the hospital mortuary. There, some prayers would be said and then the hearse would lead the cortège home. If it was any other day, I would have travelled with him. The bereaved family travelled in the cortège as was usual, and the funeral party arrived at the parish church after the long journey. The deceased was to rest in the church ahead of being buried. My father didn't mention any issue on his return.

That night, I was extra busy flying out the hot whiskeys. In the middle of the rush, I was shocked to see the sacristan from the church come through the door of the pub. This lady was not a drinker and she never went into any of the pubs. She called me aside and told me that she urgently needed to see my father. I ran upstairs to get him to come down, while people still waiting impatiently at the bar were shouting at me to come back and serve them.

As things settled in the bar, I went over to her while she waited for my father to come downstairs. She explained to me that as she was locking up the church, she thought she could hear a noise coming from the coffin at the top of the church. She also said that she thought there was a liquid leaking from the bottom of the coffin. At that point, my father had arrived on the scene. He managed to calm her down and told her that he had heard of this happening before. He assured her that he would try calling a few funeral directors to see if anyone knew what to do.

First, he called Gallagher's (run by the Foley family) in Sligo, largest of all of the funeral directors in the county, about twenty-five miles away. He also rang Miko Browne, who had a large business in Ballina, another nearby town. The advice he got was to get the deceased embalmed, and he was given the number of Billy Doggert in Belfast. Billy was a funeral director, and one of the few embalmers in the entire country. In Ireland it was not a well-known or often-used process then. We phoned him and he agreed to send one of his embalmers to us. At that time, the journey from Belfast took the best part of five hours, but it felt like much longer as we waited for him that night.

Billy's embalmer came and looked after the problem. The noise would have been caused by gas causing the body to expand, which is a very serious problem. He embalmed the deceased that night. The person had to be laid out in a different habit, and it was also necessary to change the coffin as the original one had been destroyed.

To tell the truth, we knew very little about embalming at that time, but we were very relieved that the process could solve such a terrible problem. This whole experience was to be hugely influential in my decision to pursue a career in embalming and funeral directing.

It wasn't just laying out the deceased that I was interested in and wanted to know more about – it was far more than that. It was the fulfilment I got from being able to help people when they were down and at their most helpless. But bear in mind that despite this, I was still a young man in my late teens at the time. I liked to go out with my friends and have fun with them on a night out. Sometimes the burden was heavy as I set off with them when I was aware of the sadness bestowed on a family in the area because of a death. These things preyed on my young mind, but I could not share them with my friends – firstly, out of respect for the dead, but secondly, because it wasn't really what a group of young friends wanted to talk about as they sought dates with other young people that they fancied!

Maybe I was quieter on those nights than normal.

One of the things that used to bother me was how most people referred to the deceased as 'the corpse'. That was part of the language around funerals, and probably people didn't give it much thought. Over the years, though, I have come to despise that term. It is such a stark and harsh way of referring to what is left behind after death and, for me, relates more to an object rather than to a person who was greatly loved and will be missed terribly by those who were bereaved by their passing. Some might disagree with me, but that's how I feel about it.

As I REACHED my twenties, unemployment and emigration were hitting Ireland with a bang. Easkey lost half of its senior Gaelic football team and a soccer team in the space of twelve months, as the players moved to Boston. If there was a Little Italy in New York, there was a big Easkey in Boston for sure.

I continued to work in the bar and carry out funerals, but I wanted to find out if there was any place I could study the profession of funeral directing in depth. Many years before the internet, this wasn't a particularly easy question to find the answer to. On the one hand, our traditions around death had carried on hardly changed for centuries.

But when we'd had the terrible problem that Billy Doggert had helped us with, I had seen that there was more to it, and that science had a role to play.

Summertime in Easkey always saw an influx of tourists from Northern Ireland, and fishermen were particularly interested in fishing for salmon in Easkey. As chance would have it, I was chatting a man from the north who was a customer in the bar in the evenings. His name was Lesley Simpson. In the course of the conversation, I discovered that he was a salesman for funeral requisites, and so he knew a lot of people in the business in the north. He told me that there was a correspondence course for embalmers accredited by the British Institute of Embalmers, but that it was crucial to get a work placement with a large funeral firm to learn the practical skills.

He gave me contact details for Henry Doggert, brother of Billy Doggert. Henry had an embalming school in Newtownards that was approved by the British Institute of Embalmers.

A Belfast man called Charlie Rodgers brought me to Belfast in his car to meet Henry, as travelling in a car registered in the Republic of Ireland wasn't the best idea at that time, due to the Troubles. I had got to know him from the bar and from fishing with him; he loved Easkey.

Henry showed me around their coffin-manufacturing facility and then gave me details about his embalming course, which was mainly theoretical. It was necessary for students to find their own placements with funeral firms where they could work on the practical side of the course under the supervision of a qualified embalmer. Henry had teamed up with Val O'Connor in Cork, he told me, and a course had been organised there the previous year. Henry accepted my application to do his course, and recommended that I go to Val to seek a placement with him also.

My mother was very supportive and helped me write the letter to Val O'Connor to see if he would take me under his wing as I learned the practical side of things in his mortuary. He replied to my letter, inviting me to meet him in his funeral home in Cork. I then contacted my uncle Martin Hallinan and his wife Eileen, who were living in Youghal at the time, and they told me I was welcome to stay with them. Eileen was a nurse in Cork, and she came with me to meet Val for the first time. Fortunately, after interviewing me, Val accepted me as a student.

I would be required to go to Cork for a few weeks at a time at least every two months. This arrangement suited me, as it allowed me to return home between visits and work to raise enough funds to keep me going. This became my routine over the next year or so. Eileen gave me huge help with my studies and had an excellent way of helping me to break down the modules on anatomy. Prior to this I'd been making trips to Newtownards for the theoretical course. Northern Ireland was a very troubled place to be visiting back then, and I quickly learned to keep my head down and get on with the task in hand any time I had to go there for tuition with Henry. Henry was a great tutor and had his whole course recorded on tape for his students.

I qualified as an embalmer in 1984 and framed my certificate with pride.

I didn't have to spend long with Val to find out that he was a true gentleman, totally dedicated to providing a professional funeral service to the people of Cork. He was ahead of his time. He offered me work periodically in his funeral home at North Gate Bridge in Cork. Eileen and my uncle Martin were so kind, and welcomed me into their home any time I came to Cork to work for the O'Connors after that.

I was fortunate enough to work with Val O'Connor over a number of years. I have very fond memories of him and his lovely staff, who were so kind to me. There was a vibrant atmosphere under his leadership, and the environment there was like a home away from home for me. His enthusiasm for his work and professionalism influenced me in many ways. He made me realise that there is far more to directing a funeral than merely owning and driving a hearse. He gave me sound business guidance, and his kindness towards the bereaved was infectious. His eagerness to help promote higher standards in funerals became embedded in my psyche. He always paid utmost attention to detail in how the deceased looked and was presented in the coffin.

He used to walk in front of the hearse, leading the funeral in the truest sense of a funeral director. He oozed confidence in all that he did, in a pleasant way, and this in turn led to the bereaved trusting him. He also had an excellent rapport with his staff. He had been the first funeral director to open a funeral home in the country in 1967 – he was a leader in his profession and a very inspirational man.

Very little was known about the scientific side of death here in Ireland, let alone better ways of presenting our dead. I was very much alone in my quest for knowledge in this area, and am forever grateful to Val for his support and tuition at that time. Importantly, he had studied mortuary science in America, where there was a huge focus on the presentation of the deceased. He knew that it would be good for me to go there to further my studies, and explained the vast opportunities available in the United States for gaining experience of working with myriad people from different cultural backgrounds. With a much larger population, there was also a higher chance of encountering all kinds of medical issues, which could potentially affect how the embalmer approached his or her work. He told me that seeing these first-hand, and having the opportunity to work under the guidance of experts, was the ultimate learning experience.

So I began my quest to find a suitable college in America. Val gave me some trade journals from the States and I duly wrote off to some of the colleges advertised to find out what was required to get a place on a course there. I was thrilled when different colleges wrote back to me, and I realised that my certification from secondary school and my qualification from the British Institute of Embalmers would meet the entry requirements for most of them.

Having perused all the prospectuses sent to me, I decided to apply to the Worsham College of Mortuary Science in Chicago. Students at the college were able to gain experience through the embalming and preparing of unclaimed deceased persons for Cook County morgue. I figured that at Worsham College, I would be likely to get excellent practical tuition and experience. The course involved one year of theory and one year of practical training in an apprenticeship.

I waited in anticipation for a response from Worsham College, and I vividly remember the day that letter came with the airmail sticker and the American stamps with the price marked in cents. I had been offered a place.

I knew this was where I needed to go. However, at a time when lots of my contemporaries were crossing the Atlantic for the economic opportunities, many thought I was mad going to America to be a poor student when I could go and work there instead and make my fortune.

I worked really hard in the months leading up to my trip to Chicago. At that time, I was embalming for funeral directors in a large area from the West of Ireland to the Midlands. I had to save up a lot of money so that I would be able to support myself over there. I also hoped to get work in Chicago to help with fees and my keep. Many's the night I worked hard in the bar, waiting for the last swallow and words of wisdom from the well-inebriated, well-intentioned customers, before setting off on a one- or two-hour journey into the night to work for another three hours embalming, often in very crude and basic circumstances.

I applied to education bodies here in Ireland looking for grant aid to support me in my studies, but, at that time, there was little available to those following a different career path. And nor, at that time, were grants allocated for studying abroad. I put my case forward that there was no such course here so I had no choice and begged for an exception to be made, but to no avail.

As the date to leave approached, I was both anxious and excited. Like many from my village who had left before me, I faced a whole new world. Many of my friends had gone to Boston and New York, and it would have been easier to be going out to a community of Irish who were from the same area and were very supportive of each other. Getting a job might have been easier, for one. But instead, I was going to Chicago, where I knew nobody.

I was in regular contact with the registrar at the college, who would be responsible for helping me to get settled as a foreign student. We communicated through letters and, at a later stage, she made some phone calls. If I was unlucky enough to miss the call, I would have to call back. Phone calls to America at that time were terribly expensive, so conversations with this lady were short in the lead-up to my trip to Chicago.

I explained to her that I had no family or friends in Chicago and didn't have a place to stay, either. She told me that sometimes funeral homes contacted the college looking for live-in students to work for a small wage in return for their accommodation. She arranged accommodation for me at one of these funeral homes. All this sounded fine to me, as I was so excited to have been offered a place in this college in the first place. Getting accommodation sorted was a huge relief and I was never afraid of work, so I didn't give this another thought.

There was a delay leaving as there were so many young people wanting to work in America at that time due to the lack of jobs at home that there was a backlog in getting the right paperwork. I was worried about missing the beginning of the course, but was assured that I would be able to catch up.

The registrar had told me that she would meet my flight and bring me to my accommodation on arrival. That was a comfort to me as I put my suitcase into the boot of the car and set off for Shannon Airport. Chicago was a huge city, very different to anywhere I had ever been, and I felt I would really struggle to get to my accommodation if left to my own devices. Still, there were knots in my stomach as we got closer to the airport. It was exciting to be going on a plane to America, but it was really scary not knowing what was ahead for me.

I checked in my suitcase and went through security. There was no immigration facility in Shannon Airport at that time for the United States, so I wandered around the duty-free, looking at lots of green Irish souvenirs, shamrocks, harps and shillelaghs, to while away the time as I waited until it was time to board.

When I got on the plane, I was seated right in the middle of a row, and the people either side of me promptly occupied the armrests on my seat! It was still exciting for me to be on a long-haul flight, and have food and drinks served to me. With a long flight ahead, I managed to let my seat back and sleep for a few hours.

There were no direct flights to O'Hare Airport in Chicago from Shannon. Instead, I had to catch a connecting flight at Logan International Airport in Boston. When I arrived there, however, I was delayed by several hours getting through immigration. But I had no way of telling the college registrar, who was already on her way to O'Hare Airport with her daughter. All I could do was nervously sit in immigration, not knowing what was going to happen next, having missed my flight to Chicago.

I eventually got through immigration and the airline got me on another connecting flight that was due to arrive at O'Hare Airport at 2am. Some things were a lot easier back in those days, when personnel weren't hindered by computers, so airlines did their best to help their passengers get to their destinations, even if unexpected delays had caused them to miss a flight. But still, as I got on the plane, I had no idea of what I was going to do when I got to Chicago. What would the registrar do when she arrived to find no sign of me? Would she just give up and go home?

On the flight, I was sitting next to an elderly lady from Cleveland who was going to Chicago to visit family. She laughed when I said I was from Ireland, as she said she could tell from my accent. I wasn't even aware I had an accent! I told her of my predicament. She was a lovely woman and made me feel at ease. She even gave me her address and phone number, telling me to call if I was ever in Cleveland. She also told me that she had a really good friend who was a funeral director and would help me out if I was stuck. I remember thinking that if everyone in the US was as nice as this lady, then I had landed on my feet.

As the plane touched down in Chicago, my name was announced on the passenger announcement system, and the flight attendant told me that there would be a lady waiting for me in the airport, giving me directions to where she would be. I felt a huge sense of relief.

I was in awe of the huge airport but managed to find the registrar and her daughter waiting patiently for my arrival. It turned out that when there was no sign of me in arrivals, the registrar had enquired with the airline and was told that I had boarded the first flight from Ireland, but that if I had been delayed in immigration, I could either be sent back to Ireland if my papers weren't in order, or, alternatively, they would ensure I was on the next flight to Chicago. They assured her that they would contact her if I was going to be on an onward flight to O'Hare. She duly got a call at 9pm telling her that I was scheduled to arrive in O'Hare airport at 2am, but she had no way of passing on this information to me.

It felt really cold when we stepped out of the airport. The temperature was much lower than our warmer-than-normal September in Ireland that year. I was soon to learn about the 'wind chill' in Chicago, and how you feel cooler than the actual temperature due to the breeze coming from Lake Michigan.

When we got to the car, I asked if I should put my suitcase in the boot. They both gave me a puzzled look. They didn't know what I meant. When I pointed to the back of the car, they realised I was talking about what they called the trunk.

We arrived after 3am at the funeral home in downtown Chicago where I was to be living and working. Despite the early hour, I was greeted by Kevin, another student from my class, who was to become a great friend to me. He told me that I should get a good sleep after my long journey and meet the owner in the morning. He had a car and told me that I would be able to travel to college with him each day.

I slept soundly that night and met the owner the following morning.

The owner brought me into his office. I couldn't help noticing all of the pictures of his family in expensive frames on his desk. I didn't realise that it was normal practice in the States to fill one's office with family photos.

This was also the office used to make funeral arrangements with families. He told me that on return from college each day, in the late afternoon, I would be required to don my suit and attend any repose going on in the funeral home. The repose took place in a dedicated room, where the coffin or casket was placed. The bereaved sat in the room with the deceased, and friends and relatives came to offer their condolences. A repose could last two or three hours, depending on what the bereaved wanted. Sometimes a repose was busy with people constantly coming and going, and at other times it could be quiet, with small numbers arriving at different times throughout. Following the repose, all floors had to be vacuumed and the toilets cleaned. I would then be answering the phones most nights, taking details if any calls came in. This effectively meant you couldn't leave the building. The pay was $30 per week for six days' work, but I had my accommodation too, albeit pretty rough and basic. The fridge was by the bed and the shower was in the corner of the room. The toilet was also in the bedroom, a bit like in a prison cell! The colour scheme was dreary to say the least, and it was dark even on the brightest day. There was a kitchen downstairs, with dated facilities.

The next morning began with my new friend and I setting off for college. Unfortunately, we had car trouble, which delayed us, resulting in us being an hour late. Needless to say, we were called into the president's office after classes that day to be reprimanded and reminded that punctuality was absolutely essential in our chosen career. The delay in the president's office, in turn, led to us getting another reprimand in the funeral home as we were both late returning to our work placement that afternoon!

My first day at college was daunting for me. At twenty-five, I was older than most of the other students there, some of whom hadn't long left high school. There were some students like me who had to self-fund their education, and they would have to seek a job in a funeral home after qualifying, but many in my class were sons and daughters of funeral business owners, and were therefore able to work in their home businesses at weekends and holiday periods. Their families wanted to give them the best education, and they had much more money at their disposal than any students in Ireland at that time. It was so different for me to see students who owned their own cars and had a totally different lifestyle.

Being the only foreign student in my class, I quickly became known as 'Irish'. It wasn't in any way insulting – Irish people were well liked in Chicago. My accent became the source of a lot of humour for my classmates. Firstly, they didn't understand what I was saying and, secondly, they used totally different words for some things.

A few days into the course, I quickly realised that the other students had all done a two-year preparatory course prior to starting this one. Not only had I missed the first month of the course, but I also had serious catching-up to do on the basics. It was a thorough course and included modules on anatomy, physiology, psychology, chemistry, embalming, English, restorative art (people rather than paintings!), marketing, funeral service laws and ethics, business, grief counselling, cremation, accounting, and pathology. There was a lot to learn, and I was dismayed to find out I was already behind.

I thought I had left playing catch-up with my studies behind me when I'd finished school in Ireland. When my parents had bought the pub in Easkey in 1974, they'd thought it would be more convenient to have me move to the nearest secondary school, as it meant I would be able to help out in the business after school. They didn't consider the subject mismatch that I had to face when I was landed into senior-cycle classes of subjects I had never studied before. Subjects that I had been doing really well at in my previous school weren't available in my new school.

My father wasn't very sympathetic about this. I recall clearing out a small, unused room over the pub as I wanted to use it to study, but I soon realised there was no electricity in it. I asked my mother if we could get an electrician in to put light in the room and a socket for a heater, but of course, in our house, that kind of thing was my father's decision. When I asked him, he told me that it would be a waste of electricity. I was gutted and deeply hurt by this remark. I will never forget how low I felt that day. I knew the odds were stacked against me, but I persevered without his support.

So here I was in Chicago, once again playing catch-up with my studies. I had invested everything in this course and giving up wasn't an option. I had to keep my head down and get on with it, just as I had done when I had changed school back in Ireland almost a decade earlier.

As time went by, it was difficult to listen to other students talking of their socialising at the weekends when I didn't have a social life at all between work and study. That first semester was tough, and I often looked up at my suitcase sitting on top of the wardrobe. I was very close to packing it up and going home on a few occasions. I was doing the course I really wanted to do, and loved it, but surviving as a foreign student was very hard at that time in Chicago. I don't know what force kept me going through this period, but I sure am glad that the high wardrobe made it inconvenient for me to grab that case at those times when I felt like giving up.

Not having a social life felt like a hardship for someone of my age, but the biggest problem was that I was really unhappy with my work placement. It involved a lot of work, and yet I could only just about survive on the measly $30 a week I received for all my efforts. It's no wonder that I lost a lot of weight at that time, though I was so preoccupied with everything else that I didn't even notice.

Even though my accommodation was quite sparse, and cold, it was better than nothing – but that is all I could say in its favour. Kevin and I worked long hours in that place, and the owner took full advantage of our student status and the fact that we were dependent on the accommodation he'd given us. I asked for a raise more than once, to help me to get by in consideration of the long hours I was working, but my requests fell on deaf ears. I found myself working there every hour I wasn't at college, struggling to get time to study too. I longed for a better placement, and better accommodation, but there was never time to search.

I was also getting impatient to get some work assisting in the embalming room. I had come to Chicago as a qualified and experienced embalmer, eager to learn more about my craft and develop my skills further. That was one of the main reasons I was there, but it seemed there was little or no chance of this in the funeral home I was in. For starters, the owner didn't employ full-time embalmers. Instead, he hired freelance embalming staff, who arrived, did their work, and left promptly. They had little interest in sharing any of their knowledge or skills with us students, as this might potentially delay them in their work. So, more often than not, I wasn't even permitted in the embalming room. Instead of doing what I had come to do, I was cleaning the funeral home, supervising wakes and answering phones. This was turning out to be a disaster. I knew of fellow students who were being allowed to assist embalmers at this stage in their placements with different firms.

Worsham College didn't begin their module in Cook County morgue until after Christmas. It felt like it was going to be an eternity before I would be allowed to embalm again.

It was a very lonely and disheartening time for me. I had a few good experiences, however, that incentivised me to keep going, and made me realise that there were lots of good people around me in that city. One such experience was towards the end of October. I was supervising a wake in the funeral home one evening. This involved ensuring that the bereaved had everything they needed as they sat with the deceased in the visitation room. A bell alerted me when someone came into the foyer. I had to greet any visitors and show them into the visitation room. In between callers, I tried to get some studying done in the office.

At one point, when I responded to the bell that evening, I was greeted by a policeman who was on the beat along our street. He had come in to get a drink of water from the water fountain in the foyer. He was a friendly kind of guy and spoke to me. As he didn't appear to need any further assistance, I decided to go back to my studies in the office.

As I turned around, I happened to notice that he was wearing a holster with a gun. I had never seen a gun in a holster in real life, and it brought mixed feelings of fear coupled with wonder. I was full of questions and he immediately picked up on my Irish accent. He enquired as to what part of Ireland I was from, and was excited when I told him that Ballina, County Mayo, was the nearest shopping town to my home. He told me his mother was from Laherdane, which was also near Ballina.

A few weeks later, the policeman made contact with me again and brought me to his home, where I met his mother, Mary Gleeson, and she took me under her wing. She was so kind to me, as were all of her family, and wrapped me in the love of her family circle. After that, I was often invited out to her home for meals, and she'd have her favourite recordings of Irish songs sung by John McCormack playing in the background. When the weather got colder, she sorted me out with some good warm sweaters and jackets, which were more appropriate for a cold Chicago winter. I will never forget her kindness. I became very good friends with her family and, in particular, with her son Shawn, the policeman, and his girlfriend. We had good times together. In fact, he was later to be the best man at my wedding!

Through this family, I discovered the vibrant Irish community that was in Chicago at that time. I met really lovely people and, using what little time I could spare after work and study, I volunteered in the Irish American Center that was being renovated at the time. There was great enthusiasm there and everyone was doing their bit, helping with the renovation of the centre. A very prominent figure at that time was Maureen O'Looney, who hosted the long-running *American Irish Radio Network* programme on a local Chicago radio station, which would keep us up to date with news and the latest music releases from home. She was so passionate about helping Irish immigrants, matching them with jobs and accommodation, and developing a social centre to celebrate the Irish culture in every form. I loved my encounters with the people I met at the centre, and I would return to my placement with little nuggets of hope for better times ahead.

When winter came, the heavy snowfalls set in. I had to get up at 6am each day to clear the snow from the funeral home paths and the car park across the road before going to college. Snow from the paths had to be blown towards the road in time for the bigger snowploughs to clear it away by 7am. The owner made sure I knew how to operate the snowblower. This machine was novel and fun to me when I first used it, but clearing the snow in the car park each day was to become my most hated task.

I had been used to outdoor work from working in the family business, but I had never experienced such pain in my hands. The sub-zero temperatures of Chicago felt even more brutal with the additional wind chill factored in. I had never experienced temperatures lower than minus five

Celsius in Ireland, whereas in Chicago, temperatures could reach minus twenty, and I'm amazed I never got serious frostbite!

I remember one evening taking a shower before leaving my accommodation. I generally let my hair dry naturally. On this day, it was really freezing. I went out on to the street and spotted the bus coming towards my stop, so I ran towards it. When I got on the bus, the driver and passengers at the front started to giggle. The driver told me that I should go home and dry my hair. At that point, I realised that my wet hair had frozen and was spiked on my head. My appearance was a little bit like the maverick scientist Doc Brown from the film *Back to the Future* that had come out around that time. Little did that driver know that I didn't have the luxury of a hairdryer where I was staying. I knew better the next time I washed my hair not to go out onto the street until it had dried!

It was inevitable that I would be spending my Christmas in Chicago. I was struggling to eat on the $30 a week, let alone save for a trip home. I asked my arrogant host if he could give me some more money, but he refused as usual, and promptly reminded me that I was only a 'stoodent'.

Things were subsequently to change for the better for me, though, in a most unexpected manner.

It was as though something stronger was guiding the way.

Ginny

ONE DAY IN EARLY December, I had just arrived at college when I noticed a gathering of my class group around a noticeboard. Being smaller than most of the members of my class, I decided to wait until they had moved to find out what had attracted their attention. I had to go for a grind (extra tuition) and on my return, the others had all gone home. I went over to the noticeboard. They had been looking at an advertisement for a live-in student in one of the finest funeral homes in Chicago at that time.

I had heard talk of this place among the students. The funeral home had a large geographical catchment in the city, incorporating very diverse spiritual and religious traditions. The funeral business had just been acquired by SCI (Service Corporation International), which I knew was one of the biggest funeral companies in the States and the world. Jobs there were highly sought after by students, as it was known that quality experience and training would be guaranteed. Staff were well looked after and, of course, there was live-in accommodation. I took down the details and resolved that I would at least attend for interview.

On the Friday, I remember asking for three hours off work the next day so I could go to the interview for the job with the other company – although, of course, I didn't tell my boss where I was going. My request was reluctantly granted on condition that my student colleague covered for me. Kevin was good enough to oblige, and delayed the journey home for Christmas that he had planned.

I put on my best clothes, with the address of the other funeral home jotted on a bit of paper in my pocket. I asked a few people for directions, but decided to take a taxi in case I got lost and ended up being late for the interview. I had been working so much that my knowledge of Chicago amounted to the route from the funeral home to the college, and the few places my friends had taken me.

When the taxi driver pulled up at the address I had given him, a journey of about forty minutes, I was sure there was a mistake as it looked like a very grand hotel. I disputed with the driver and explained that I needed to go to a funeral home. He pointed to the funeral home sign at the entrance and then demanded his fare of $15. I had my week's wages in my pocket, so I thought that at least I would have the fare back afterwards. However, he demanded a tip. There wasn't a culture of tipping in Ireland back then. You just paid what you were asked and that was the deal done. But this taxi driver roared at me about having a family to feed. I eventually conceded and gave him a tip in order to get out of what was becoming a very embarrassing situation. This left me with just $10 for my homeward trip.

I was very shaken as I made my way into the funeral home, following the altercation with the taxi driver. I couldn't get over how big the building was, with its grand entrance under an enormous canopy. It spanned a full block. When I entered, I nervously enquired as to where the interviews were being held, while hoping that nobody had heard the roars of the taxi driver outside. I was shown to an area and was surprised to see about thirty other students from the college waiting there before me. The ones I knew joked with me about not having a hope of getting the job with my Irish accent, as they would also need to hire an interpreter in order to understand what I was saying. One of them reminded me to take the potato out of my mouth before speaking. So much for boosting my confidence as I faced the first interview of my life!

I was the last in line. As I waited, I chatted with my fellow interviewees. They referred to the recent takeover by SCI and told me that the company had 600 funeral homes, 100 crematoriums and 300 flower shops across the US. This included forty funeral homes and one cemetery in Chicago alone. I was in awe. This was a huge company, and I didn't hold out much hope of getting the job. However,

I was here now, and might as well at least chalk up the experience of doing the interview, I thought.

My turn eventually came to go into the office, where two gentlemen sat on either side of a lady behind a large office desk. They were all smartly groomed. It was a dark room, and the lady, who had blonde hair and was wearing a lot of make-up, stood out as she sat in the centre. They asked me about my background and the course I was taking at Worsham College. The lady commented on my Irish accent and remarked that it might pose problems with answering phone calls.

Before the interview finished, she asked me the earliest date I could start, should I be selected for the job. I promptly replied 'tonight' without a further thought, as I knew there was nothing enticing me to stay in the other place. I thanked them for their time and they thanked me in return for coming and then showed me out.

Next, I had to negotiate my way back to where I was staying, on $10. I got some directions before leaving the funeral home, figuring that if I walked some of the way, the $10 I had left in my pocket would surely cover the taxi the rest of the way.

After walking for at least two hours, I hailed a taxi. He had no interest in taking a $10 fare including tip but told me that I hadn't much further to go, so I walked the rest of the way back.

GINNY

It had been a long way but I was so excited, having done my first interview and dreaming of getting the job, that I hadn't really noticed the time as I walked. But I soon realised that I was an hour late returning to the other funeral home. I rushed upstairs and quickly put on my funeral attire. I went straight into work. By then, the repose was nearly over. Kevin, who had delayed going home to Rock Island in order to cover for me, left as soon as I arrived. I was grateful to him and felt bad for keeping him. The owner of the funeral home had gone to a Christmas party, and I was to be on duty for the rest of the evening on my own. He said I could put the phones on to the answering service later on when I had locked up.

I was mesmerised by the events of the day. I couldn't stop thinking about the enormous funeral home. I had never seen anything like it and I longed to have a job there. I weighed up my chances of getting it, with so many of my class in against me. My chances were slim but I could at least continue to dream of getting employment there, couldn't I?

I tried to study that evening when I finished work, but was totally distracted. I glanced up at my suitcase, this time desperately hoping that I might be packing my few belongings in it to go to a new job, rather than sadly wishing I could return home, as I had a number of times in the past few months.

At around 8pm, the phone rang and I answered it as normal. The caller asked to speak to David McGowan. I told him that I was David McGowan. He asked if I was the man who had attended for the interview earlier that day and again I confirmed I was, though I was barely able to speak in shock, as I hadn't really expected a call, for all my daydreams. He reminded me that I had said that I would be able to start that night, if I was to get the job, and he wondered if that was still an option. He said that if I could get over there that night, then the job was mine. I told him that I could go over there immediately. I couldn't believe it! I got the job and I was over the moon. I looked up at my suitcase. I was moving, but not back to Ireland, as I had been contemplating earlier in the week.

I called a friend and told him what had happened. I explained that I had only $10 and wouldn't be able to afford a taxi back to my new job. He happened to be in my area and said he would be over shortly, to bring me.

I decided to call my boss to tell him I had got a new job. Someone else at the party he was at answered the phone and I could hear them calling him to the phone, saying that the 'Irish kid' wanted to talk to him. 'Hi there, Irish.' He never addressed me by my name. 'Have you a funeral call for me?' He presumed that I had received a call about a someone who had died. He was very irate when I told him that I was leaving within the hour to take up a different job and that I would be transferring the phones to the answering service a little bit earlier than expected. He shouted at me, telling me he would be talking to me in the morning, to which I replied that I was going that night. I told him I was grateful to him for giving me work and accommodation, but reiterated that I couldn't survive on $30 a week, and that he had made it clear to me on the few occasions I had asked that he would not pay me more money. I said that if I didn't take this job, I had resolved to return home anyway, as there was no way I could live on the meagre pay he was giving me.

He threatened to report me to the college. Fortunately, my achievement of getting my new job overshadowed his threat. I hadn't travelled 3,500 miles from home to answer phones, supervise reposes, vacuum floors and clear snow. My true mission in Chicago was to learn more of the art of embalming and soak up as much knowledge, both academic and practical, as I could, in my time in a city with limitless opportunities for learning. In my new job, I hoped I would be learning from full-time embalmers who cared about maintaining a high standard.

After I hung up the phone to my angry former employer, I eagerly whipped down my bag and in, less than five minutes, my few belongings were packed and I was ready to go. My friend arrived to collect me. Boy, was I happy as I flung my case into the back of his car. I was actually going to be returning to the amazing building where I had attended the interview only a few hours previously. I was elated.

My friend also couldn't believe the size of the funeral home when we arrived. His first impression was the same as mine – he too initially thought that it was a posh hotel. He helped me with my case and kindly gave me the loan of $20 to tide me over.

I entered the foyer and was greeted by two of the funeral directors who were on call. I recognised one as one of the interviewers I met earlier that day. They were very friendly and helpful.

This time, I really took notice of the vastness of this wonderful funeral home. On entry to the grand foyer, you were met with plush carpets and a welcoming fire set in a grand fireplace, over which hung a large portrait of the original owner and founder of the business. Comfortable couches were placed strategically around the foyer, for the use of mourners who wanted to chat quietly or simply just take a few moments alone. There was an elegant staircase at either end of the foyer, each disappearing from view behind the fireplace.

I was led up the staircase to the right to where I would be staying. I was told in no uncertain terms that the other staircase on the left was strictly private, and that I was not to disturb the woman who lived there.

When we reached my quarters, I was in awe of the fabulous apartment that I would be sharing with the other live-in student. There was a nice shower and toilet, and the kitchen had a large fridge that had been stocked up by the company. It was amazing and a far cry from the place I had just left. I had to pinch myself to prove it wasn't a dream.

Before the two gentlemen left me, they brought me back downstairs and gave me a brief tour of the building, showing me how to lock up, which lights to leave on all night, and giving a number to call should I need anything. They told me that I would be alone in my apartment in the building for my first few weeks, and that another student would also be staying there at a later date. I wondered if it would be another student from Worsham College.

I asked about the snowblower, presuming that I would be out early the next day, but they told me that a company was hired for that job.

Then they left. As far as I knew, I was the only living soul in the building. Although perhaps the lady who lived on the other side of the building was home. I had no way of knowing. As I turned to go back upstairs to my quarters, I passed the room I had been interviewed in earlier. I paused to look in for a moment and then proceeded upstairs. I made myself a cup of tea, sat down and tried to watch the TV, though I wasn't really paying much attention to it.

I decided to go to bed. But my brain was on overdrive and I couldn't sleep. Instead, I spent the rest of the night replaying all of the events of that extraordinary day over and over again in my mind. I could never have envisaged how it was to unfold. I asked myself how this could all have landed in my lap. What had inspired me to apply for this job, let alone get it without the help or encouragement of anyone else? It was a major boost to my self-confidence, which had reached an all-time low before that. I had a gut instinct that I was in exactly the place I needed to be. Something powerful had kept me on the path that had led me here, in spite of all of the odds being against me. It was a day that was pivotal in changing my whole experience in America and, subsequently, my life.

I waited until 7am to get up the next morning. The shower I had was the nicest since my arrival in Chicago; it was so refreshing compared with the dribble of water in the shower in my last abode. I made myself a coffee and then ventured out of my apartment. On my floor, there was even a restaurant area for patrons. What luxury.

It was Sunday and two other funeral directors were already on duty. They welcomed me and we chatted.

I asked them about the embalming theatre. After so long not having had any practice in the area I was already trained and hoping to develop my skills in, I was itching to get started and desperately hoping I would be allowed to start assisting the embalmers soon. Surely in an establishment of this calibre I'd be able to learn from the best? I don't know if they were amused by my enthusiasm, but they told me that I would be told all that by the manager when he came in.

The branch manager arrived promptly at 9am and joined us. He told me to follow him as we proceeded on a tour around the entire building. Throughout the tour, there was huge emphasis on security, lights, alarms and ensuring that doors were kept locked. I was given keys for the main entrance and the back entrance, where staff usually entered the building and ambulances entered with the deceased. There were security cameras around the building and car park. Attention was paid to fire escapes and ensuring that they were kept clear at all times. I was slightly surprised that they were so security conscious, but I didn't really question it as I was so focused on taking in my new responsibilities. What I hadn't understood – being new to Chicago – was that we were in an area where the 'Outfit' was active. This branch of the Mafia had evolved during the early twentieth century and, of course, had Italian roots. Gang wars had become common in order to gain control of the distribution of illegal alcohol during prohibition. The 'Outfit' evolved into the most powerful, violent and largest criminal organisation in Chicago, continuing in crime long after the prohibition period ended. Not that I had any clue about this!

I eagerly asked about seeing the embalming facilities, but the manager told me that was at the back of the building and he wanted to talk me through the security of the building first. I was also shown the visitation rooms and told everything that was expected of me when a wake was taking place.

The tour of my new workplace led us up to the main office. I noticed lots of pictures around the place, including a photograph of Mayor Daley, the famous and very powerful Chicago mayor of the 1950s, 60s and 70s, standing alongside the original owner of the business. The branch manager sat me down and gave me a list of duties that I was to carry out in the funeral home. My main responsibilities were to help with wakes and look after security, checking that all was locked up each evening, and that certain lights were left on at night. The manager also reiterated that I was not to go up the other flight of stairs to where the lady lived. He mentioned briefly that she worked for the company, and said she would be coming and going and that I wasn't to disturb her.

Finally, we left the office and I was shown the embalming theatre. There were six embalming tables and six dressing tables, all in use, a trolley for cosmetics and another for hair-styling equipment. The two embalmers and the hairdresser working there introduced themselves to me. I was happy to see that the way they embalmed was similar to the way I had been shown in Cork, though I was blown away by the sheer scale of the mortuary area. I knew I belonged here. The manager told me that even though I was qualified in Ireland, there was a strict licensing system in America. Unions ensured that this was adhered to and until, I was licensed, I couldn't embalm on my own. I could, however, assist embalmers with dressing, etc.

I was busy that day, getting familiar with my new job. I assisted the funeral directors with the four wakes that were taking place that evening, carefully noting anything they told me to do. When the last of the families was leaving, I began cleaning up the foyer and visitation room. The other funeral director told me that cleaners would look after that in the morning. He made very sure I had locked up everything before he left.

I was on my own again. I couldn't resist the temptation of going back to the embalming area for another look. It was an amazing place, like nothing I had ever seen before. I must have spent about an hour in that Aladdin's cave, full of awe and curiosity. Every piece of equipment that an embalmer could possibly need was there at your fingertips. It was unbelievable. A total of six deceased people had been embalmed there that Sunday, with another ten lined up for the next day. This was what I had come to the United States for. I was so excited to have the opportunity of working in this mortuary, albeit only assisting until I was licensed.

The timing of this change of job was perfect too. College had finished until after Christmas, giving me a great chance to settle in and learn the ropes.

As I headed up to the apartment that I would have to myself for the next few weeks, I thought about how bizarre it was to be alone in a building with so many deceased people, and this mystery woman in her apartment on the other side of the building, whom I hadn't yet met. I was very content and happy to be there, though.

After a good night's sleep, I arose the next morning bright and early at 7am, eager to begin work. I arrived downstairs to the hum of vacuuming. The cleaners were almost finished as I began opening. This was so different to my last job. By 7am, I would have just finished blowing snow from the car park and would be trying to warm up my painful frozen hands.

I had been instructed to check on all of our 'guests' in their comfortable caskets, to ensure that they still looked their best, so I went to take a look. I then met with the four funeral directors on duty that day, who would be looking after the funerals that morning. I assisted them, observing their way of doing things and following their instructions with as much precision as I could possibly manage.

After they had left in the hearses, I made my way to the mortuary. I was greeted by the embalmers, who were gowned up and busy with their work. I offered to help and, after I had assisted them with dressing one deceased man, they realised that they could trust me to dress the other deceased people when they had finished their embalming work. Throughout the day, more deceased people were brought in for preparation, and others were removed respectfully in their caskets to different funeral homes. This embalming facility was used by twenty funeral homes in the SCI group, so it was really busy there all day.

At 6pm, I reluctantly left the embalming area to go and assist with the three wakes that were taking place in the visitation rooms out front.

GINNY

As with the previous evening, the last of the bereaved had left by 9pm and it was time to lock up again, as staff all headed home. As per my instructions, I switched on the night lights and checked all doors, though once again I couldn't resist having one quick peep at the embalming area before heading upstairs.

It was late by then, and so I was startled to find a lady with blonde hair busy attending to the make-up and hair of a deceased lady. She was shocked too! As she introduced herself, I instantly recognised her as the lady who had interviewed me for the job. Her name was Virginia Lucania, and I would get to know her as 'Ginny'. She asked me how I was settling in. As she talked to me, I put two and two together and realised that she was the mystery woman living on the other side of the building! I asked if I could stay for a little while and see how she did the hair of the deceased lady. She said there was no problem at all and that I could stay.

That was to mark the beginning of my training with the most skilled person working in death care that I have ever met in my life. She didn't just present a person well, she put her heart and soul into every last detail, while spiritually engaging with the deceased. She was a perfectionist. I was fascinated. As she worked, she talked to the deceased lady as if she was alive. I had never seen anyone do that before. There was something very nice about it, though, and I thought of all of the bereaved and how lucky they were to have entrusted their loved ones to her genuine care.

I helped her to dress two other ladies, and she spoke to them too as she did their hair and make-up. We didn't finish until midnight, but I hadn't felt the time passing at all. I knew that this lady had unique skills, and I wanted to learn from her. It seemed that she only worked in the mortuary when all of the embalmers had gone home, although it wasn't quite clear why.

We finished up in the mortuary and parted company in the foyer as we ascended our stairs to our separate abodes.

THE WEEK CONTINUED in this fashion – opening up in the morning, helping the funeral directors with removals, assisting in the mortuary until 6pm, wakes in the evening, and back to the mortuary to learn more about the finishing touches. I never presumed that I would be welcome in the mortuary and always asked Ginny for permission before entering. We seemed to be getting along well, but I sensed that she would not hesitate to expel me from the mortuary if she had any problem with my work, and I was always cautious and respectful in the way that I spoke to her.

Ginny was so talented at doing the correct hairstyle for each person, as well as meticulously attending to cosmetics and overall presentation of the deceased. By the end of that first week, she had showed me her method for putting rollers in hair, blow-drying the hair, and even how to colour it. I was over the moon to be learning all of this from an expert. She kept drilling it into me that the presentation of the deceased was of utmost importance. Even combing hair the wrong way could have disastrous consequences for the way a person appeared, and could render them unrecognisable to their loved ones. The more I learned, the more I realised just how much there was to learn!

By the end of the week, I plucked up the courage to ask Ginny why she preferred to work alone in the mortuary after the embalmers had gone home, and also why she talked to the deceased in such a fond and friendly way.

After a few uncomfortable moments of silence, she told me that this had been her family's business for years. It had been sold to SCI, but they had agreed that the original owners would continue to manage the funeral home their way, for the most part, over the coming years. The funeral home was located in a vibrant community that was predominantly of Italian descent. This was Ginny's community – when someone passed away and came into the funeral home, often Ginny would have known them. These people had been her friends and neighbours, and she cared about them. The families knew in turn that when they requested Ginny's services personally, their loved one would get her first-class attention, care and respect.

She trusted the staff with the embalming side of things and generally focused on the finishing touches – doing the make-up, hair and overall presentation in the casket. However, she was still extremely particular, believing that good embalming was futile if it wasn't coupled with equally good presentation. She was very interesting to talk to, and I always learned something new from her. We continued working most nights until 10 or 11pm.

An Unusual Christmas

TIME PASSED QUICKLY. By the second week, I'd got to know all of the staff, from branch manager to funeral directors, embalmers, florists, secretaries, cleaners and even workers from the company that regularly delivered the caskets. It was a hive of activity from morning till night, and I loved every minute of it – a far cry from the other funeral home that had now become a distant memory. Then, Christmas was almost upon us.

I was still curious as to why I had got the job. When I went to receive my first pay cheque, the manager told me that the reason I been chosen over the other thirty students was that none of them were prepared to start work until after the holidays. The company urgently needed someone to do security and be onsite in the building over the Christmas period, so I had been in the right place at the right time!

When I looked at my pay cheque, I was shocked to discover that I was to be paid $350 each week. What a difference from $30! Life was truly looking up for me, and I couldn't have been happier.

The branch manager asked me if I was OK to work over the entire holiday period, including Christmas Day. I told him I hadn't any plans and I would be happy to work over the holidays. He thanked me for my good will.

On Christmas Day, I was on duty with two funeral directors and two embalmers. It started out as a normal day. Five funeral calls had come in during the night, but all had died in hospitals, rather than at home. I was asked if I would go in the ambulance to assist one of the funeral directors when he went to collect the deceased. With little to no traffic on the streets, and it being Christmas Day, we had the first three people collected in no time. We then had to head Downtown for the remaining two. By the time we got back, the two embalmers had two of the first three deceased persons embalmed. It was decided that a break had been well earned, and that we should have our Christmas dinner.

We ordered six pizzas and spent almost two hours chatting as we ate. The others were from different backgrounds, but all four were Vietnam veterans. I found their stories very interesting and some really sad. I learned that they had all wanted to pursue medical careers prior to the war, but by the time they had returned from Vietnam, the prospect of spending at least four years in college was not so attractive for young men who were anxious to get on with their lives. They also had to cope with the terrible psychological effects the war had had on them. They had been surrounded by death, so they decided to explore the possibility of becoming embalmers, because the work was still in the medical field and it would take them less time to qualify.

They asked me if I lived anywhere near the Troubles in my country. They thought Dublin was all of Ireland, so there was little point in trying to explain to them where I was actually from in the country.

We had a very interesting and enjoyable afternoon over our unusual Christmas dinner of pizzas!

When we returned to our work in the mortuary, I remarked that three of the deceased people we had collected that day were from the local area, and so Ginny might want to look after their hair and cosmetics. The others were puzzled as to who had told me about her and how I knew her name. They had no idea that I had already met Ginny, and they didn't know I had worked with her in the evenings. They quickly noted that she was away for the holidays, but I was able to tell them she would be back the next day.

I got the impression that they didn't want to contact her.

I knew by then that she had the reputation of being absolutely meticulous with her work, and she expected the same from the home's employees. She would work tirelessly until the job was finished, no matter how long that took, and she would make the embalmers redo the work if necessary. Her philosophy was that there was no point in meticulously embalming a person if the details weren't right from head to foot – if, for example, the deceased person wasn't straight in the casket, their nails weren't cleaned properly or the make-up not applied to her high standard – and likewise, there was little point in attending to the finer details if the embalmer had been careless in his or her work, potentially leading to all kinds of issues arising. There is nothing more distressing for the bereaved than an odour coming from their deceased loved one.

As far as the embalmers were concerned, however, she was a workaholic, and they didn't like to get caught working the same shift as her, as that meant longer working hours. So they dodged her whenever they could.

It seemed that Ginny had been used to leading the embalming and preparation of the deceased her way, but since the SCI takeover, she had discovered that some things needed to change, and she found that challenging at times. So, in order to dispel any differences of opinion in the mortuary, everything ran smoothly if the embalmers did their work during the day and she followed up by looking after the details of presentation each evening.

As she had told me, she would look after the deceased if relatives asked for her specifically. They asked for her because of her excellent reputation and because they had got to know her personally over the years. She ended up being called in most days.

That arrangement seemed to suit everyone, as they all ultimately wanted to maintain the standard of presentation for which the funeral home was revered.

As the embalmers finished their work, they started scrubbing down the mortuary tables. I volunteered to take over and clean up, so they could spend what was left of Christmas Day with their families. It didn't really matter to me, so I didn't mind. They were more than happy to take me up on my offer.

I didn't notice the time passing as I finished up and, all of a sudden, I realised that I had forgotten to phone home. All the same, as I climbed the stairs to my apartment, I reflected that I felt good about my day. Despite having had to work, it was nice to have had the opportunity to get to know two of the other embalmers. Christmas 1985 will remain etched in my memory forever. All had gone pretty well for me, and yet that evening, I was acutely aware of those five families who would have painful memories of that same day, having lost loved ones.

Upstairs in my apartment, I made myself some tea and picked up the phone to ring home, but nobody answered. Then it dawned on me that it was 3am back home. So, hoping I hadn't woken them up, I abandoned the call with the intention of calling earlier the next day.

My days continued in much the same manner over the Christmas period, as I assisted daily in the mortuary. I was learning so much from Ginny about the presentation and final preparation of the deceased. I was learning technique but, more importantly, she instilled in me how vital it was to be conscientious in my work. Her attention to detail was fascinating. For example, if she thought a man was very particular about the crease in his pants, she would cut a length of cardboard and slip it under the pants, lining the long edge up with the crease so that it stayed perfectly straight. This is the kind of detail I was taking note of, soaking up all this new knowledge like a sponge. She explained everything so well and encouraged me.

As the holiday period came to an end, the branch manager informed me that another student would be joining me in the apartment. He acknowledged that I had worked really hard and had given over and above for my first few weeks there. He told me that I would be able to share my current workload with the other student. It wasn't realistic for me to continue working such long hours, as I would quickly burn out – particularly now college was about to start again – and that wouldn't serve anyone's best interests.

So, towards the end of the month, I met my new roommate for the first time. When he arrived, I was asked to help him to settle in and show him what had to be done downstairs when there was a wake going on, and how to lock up in the very particular way the funeral home insisted on. I advised him to trim his extremely long and untidy beard, as it wasn't in keeping with the clean-cut staff presentation that was expected in the funeral home. I was surprised he had turned up without shaving, and told him he would probably be called into the office if he didn't attend to it immediately.

While it was nice to have company for a change, I quickly discovered that this guy never stopped talking! He would talk well into the night, and was full of questions about me, my family and Ireland. I didn't want to be rude at first, but after a few nights of very little sleep, I had to tell him to stop talking so we could get some sleep! He had a car, and was kind enough to offer to bring me to college each day. It turned out he was in my class, but what was odd about it was that I didn't recognise him. Perhaps it was the beard that he had grown over the holidays that confused me.

Going back to college that January was exciting. I had a good rapport with the staff in my new job and they were supportive of me, so I knew that I had people who would help me if there was anything I didn't understand in my lectures. I had much better conditions for studying, too. Having a second live-in student in the building also meant that I would have some more time off, not that I really cared about that.

Having said that, I did draw up a rota for us, and the manager approved it. This rota timed nicely with an opportunity to ask a girl I fancied to go on a date. I had noticed her as she often popped in to see her mom, who worked in the funeral home. I had lined up my first free evening to coincide with our first day back at college, and so arranged to go out with her that day. Things were really looking up for me, and Chicago sure was a great place to be.

The Outfit

THE NEW STUDENT quickly began to get familiar with the routines and regular tasks that had to be done in the funeral home and assisting with the wakes. However, there were a few odd things that I couldn't help but notice. For example, he came to the mortuary one evening and, as he helped me to dress the deceased, I realised that he was hopelessly awkward at the task. I would have been quicker without his help, but instead, I had to be patient and remember that he too was a student, and that I should help him as others had helped me. Still, it seemed strange to me at the time that he would have difficulty with what was a relatively easy part of the work.

I was curious as to why he had decided to take the course. He told me that he didn't have any background in the business, but his uncle owned a funeral home and had offered him a job. I was puzzled, as it wasn't a regular kind of job that everyone was comfortable doing, and this guy hadn't had anything to do with the deceased prior to that. Why had he chosen to study mortuary science, of all things?

There was also another student working with us who was starting back after the holidays, but he wasn't living in. I got to know him really well as time went on. He and his wife often invited me to join them if they were going out with friends.

I was glad to be back at college again. There was plenty of chat and catching up to do, and I quickly discovered that Kevin, my room-mate from my last placement, had also managed to get away from the stingy owner of the funeral home we'd worked in together and find somewhere new, which was good to hear. Everyone was sharing news of their holidays. Some had been working in their family funeral homes; others had had nice family breaks. When they had finished, all attention turned to me. 'Well, Irish, what did you do for the holidays?' When I divulged where I had landed a job, I was inundated with questions. They wanted to know all about the funeral home, which was renowned in the city for mobster funerals. I was surprised by their questions. In my naivety, I really hadn't a clue what they were talking about.

I didn't know what they wanted to hear, and I only had good things to say about everyone working with me in the place. One of the other two students working there part-time joined in the conversation, but I noticed that my room-mate kept a very low profile. They were all fascinated by the sheer volume of funerals that went on in the funeral home. I told them that despite the number of funerals every day, everything was very well managed and calm, and every family got the same level of attention. They wanted to know if there had been any excitement over the holidays and were disappointed to learn that I'd had a pretty mundane time, working steadily in my new workplace.

Being from the West of Ireland, I was very green to the workings of 'the Outfit' in Chicago, part of the larger Italian-American Mafia. I had no idea of how the organisation operated. But as I learned more about it, I started to realise that the other students had a point – in the funeral home I worked in, I would be likely to encounter funerals of victims of 'the Outfit', or possibly even perpetrators of crime themselves, by simple virtue of the fact that following death, there has to be a funeral! This also provided a possible explanation for why the security was so tight.

It was no wonder that I was the centre of attraction that day, and the other students couldn't believe just how green I was to that world. For example, I had no idea that the funeral of the high-profile mobster 'Sam' Giancana had taken place over a decade previously in the same funeral home that I was now working in, though it had been a big deal. I didn't even know who he was at that time.

Surely this was mainly in the past, though, and not something I could expect to see in the funeral home while I was working there . . . ?

All the exciting conversations came to an abrupt end when I was summoned to the president's office. It seemed like an eternity since I had left my first work placement, so I had forgotten about the owner's threat to report me to the college. But here I was, with the president of the college reading out a lengthy complaint that he had received from my previous boss, stating that I had walked out without giving any notice and that he would never be taking on another student from the college again. He also suggested that I be expelled from the college for such behaviour.

I explained all of my issues with the placement to the president. I recounted the long working hours – six days a week for $30 per week and all the cleaning duties and snow-clearing I'd been expected to do. I told him that I'd had little or no time for studying and, worse still, most of the time I was kept out of the embalming area. I informed him that I had come to America to improve on my skills and knowledge as an embalmer, and that I had embalmed almost 2,000 deceased persons prior to coming to study there. I was well aware of the basics, but I wanted to be better.

When I told him that I had got a job in a really large funeral home, he seemed to know already and compli- mented me on my achievement. He warned me not to leave my current work without notice, and reminded me that the college depended on the goodwill of funeral homes in order to get work for students. He didn't want any other funeral home to be upset by me. He did, however, tell me that I wasn't the first student to have had a bad experience in that place. I was told that if I walked out on my new job, I would be put out of the course and would be on the next flight home. I confirmed that I had no intention of doing so, and thanked him for his patience and understanding.

It seemed like a good opportunity to ask him if I needed to study all subjects on the course. At that juncture, I didn't realise the importance of the sociology, business, communications and psychology classes, so I asked if I could drop these in favour of spending more time on microbiology and chemistry. Chemistry was a new subject for me, and I found the level being studied hugely challenging, as a point of entry. I wanted to be able to spend more time on these subjects so I could improve.

However, the president advised against dropping any subjects, and pointed out that considering how new I was to some of them, my first semester results were quite good. All subjects were essential in America towards getting qualified, and that was necessary in order to get licensed to work there. He asked where I intended to be working after college, and I said that my dream was to go back to Ireland to open my own funeral business, but that I wasn't ruling out the possibility of staying on in America either, although that would require a whole load of extra paperwork in order to extend my visa.

The president explained that all parts of the course were interdependent and were vital for my holistic development as an embalmer *and* as a funeral director. It was vital to study the effects of death on human beings emotionally and on society as a whole.

I didn't drop any subjects, and I am glad that I took his advice, as it was all these extra subjects that helped me to understand the bigger picture of what happens when someone dies and would, in the future, help me to make important decisions when guiding the bereaved through the funeral of a loved one. It took me a while to see this, so I suppose I was green in quite a few ways back then.

I was so glad not to have been expelled and looked forward to the practical module, which was due to start in February in Cook County morgue – Cook County being the region in which the city of Chicago is found. I had read so much about the place, and I had heard there was even a film being made there at that time. From about the 1840s, when the city was growing rapidly, fuelled by speculators and business people, and subject to fast cycles of boom and bust, Cook County morgue was the place where anyone who had died in suspicious circumstances was taken. Medical students were trained there, and the process of autopsies was partly developed there. It was also where the victims of the Chicago Mafia would have been taken – but again, that was not something I knew much about at the time. I was more interested in what I was going to be able to learn from our time there.

AS MY ROOM-MATE and I travelled back to the funeral home that evening, I began to think about the girl with whom I had the arranged the date. I was looking forward to going out with her. But when we arrived back, one of the secretaries called me to one side to tell me that Ginny wanted me to work that evening, and to call her because she needed to see me privately in her office downstairs when I came in. The secretary had told her I was off-duty that evening. She winked at me, indicating that she could pretend she hadn't seen me. She shared the view that Ginny was a workaholic, and half the funeral home staff must have known about my date!

However, my curiosity got the better of me, and I couldn't resist. I still had plenty of time before my date at 9pm.

I went into Ginny's office and she closed the door before giving me my assignment for the evening. She wanted me to go to O'Hare Airport to collect a deceased person coming in on a 5pm flight from Washington DC. That sounded OK – I figured I could be back in plenty of time to get ready. I did say that I was worried that any of the other employees on duty might object to me going to the airport, as it was a job usually given to someone more experienced, quietly hoping she would call one of them instead. She told me she would deal with them if there was a problem, and that the family of the deceased were friends of hers. She wanted me to go.

I hurried off to change into my suit, and I was soon on my way to the airport. I had been there before with colleagues, though never on my own. I just saw it as a compliment that I was being trusted to go alone now.

On arrival at the airport, I followed the signs for the area where the commercial flights came in, as that was also the place where caskets were collected by funeral directors. As I drove carefully towards the gate, I couldn't help noticing five black limousines parked on the right-hand side. I hadn't seen that any other time I had been at the airport, but didn't think much more about it. I was on a mission to get this casket as soon as possible and get back in time for my date.

I talked to a man through the intercom at the gate, and he opened it, enabling me to go to the building where the casket would be. I reversed the hearse back towards the closed door and then proceeded to the office hatch with my paperwork. I rang the bell, and the man came over to the window and took the paperwork from me. He told me to wait in my vehicle, and said I would be called when the casket was ready for release. It was 7pm by now, so I said that I thought that the flight had come in two hours ago. He agreed and once more told me firmly to wait in my vehicle.

After waiting for what seemed like a long half an hour, I decided to venture over to the hatch again. The same man spoke to me through the hatch and gave me the same blank refusal. I was sent back to my vehicle a second time. I headed back over to the man in the office, resolving to plead with him to see if he could hurry things up a little bit so that I could get back for my date.

He looked at me in shock and asked if I had any idea of whom I was collecting. I told him I had just been sent to collect a deceased person, and I desperately needed to get straight back to the funeral home to get ready for my date.

'You really don't know, do you?'

This time, he opened the door and brought me into his office. From the window at the back, it was possible to view everything in the cargo area. I could see six men dressed in suits standing around a casket. He told me they were FBI agents, and they had the power to hold the casket there as long as they liked. I pleaded with him to ask them if there was any chance of speeding up the process. He reluctantly agreed to at least try. I could see him through the window, talking to the men. He returned and told me that they needed to talk to me and see my ID.

The FBI agents interviewed me, checking out my ID. After about fifteen minutes, they allowed me to reverse the hearse into the area, and they helped me load the casket.

Finally, I could be on my way with my mystery guest. As I drove through the gate, I noticed that the five limousines were still parked there. I remember thinking that was extremely odd, as that area was reserved for cargo collection, and I had only ever noticed limousines at the passenger terminal. I navigated my way out of the airport, but soon noticed that the five limousines were now driving behind me. At first, I thought it was coincidence, but as I got going on my route back to the funeral home, so too did my mysterious entourage.

Even though it wasn't long after 8pm, the entire funeral home was in darkness. I wondered if there had been some sort of power outage. The limousines pulled into the funeral home car park, but I just continued around the back with the hearse as normal.

As I reversed towards the back door, I saw Ginny waiting for me. I got out of the vehicle, and she was already opening the rear door of the hearse and beginning to take out the casket. Only a few lights were switched on. I asked where everyone else was, and she replied that she had sent everyone home early. I asked also why the lights out front were off, as they were usually on at this time of night. My question fell on deaf ears.

I was ready to make a quick exit after helping to bring the casket into the mortuary, so I said I would call my colleague upstairs to come to help. She immediately told me not to, and that the two of us would look after this man.

From the moment we opened that casket, I knew that there was going to be no date for me that night. Ginny wasn't happy with the deceased man's appearance, and that was that. I was already aware, from my short experience of working with her, that she would have no hesitation in working on that man until she was satisfied that he looked well for his family, even if it meant starting the preparation and presentation process from scratch.

I asked about my date, and she went out and called the girl's mother, explaining that she had called me in to work and that the date was off for tonight. I didn't feel as bad once she had notified the girl, as I knew she wouldn't be sitting waiting for me. I was disappointed, but at the same time I knew that I needed to stay, as it was an important opportunity to learn skills I would need in the future from my mentor.

I assisted her with the complete preparation. By the time she was finished, the difference was unbelievable. She held back tears as she worked. We kept going until after 11.30pm. When he was ready, we carefully wheeled the casket into the main visitation room.

At one stage, I heard someone trying to get into the mortuary, but Ginny must have locked the door, and whoever it was went away again.

I was tired and disappointed to have missed my date. However, that night, I had learned that a person could look totally different when embalmed and prepared by two different people with different approaches. I realised that Ginny had the advantage of knowing what the dead man had looked like in life, and she was determined to restore his appearance so that his family and friends could remember him as he had been.

She left me to clean up in the mortuary. When I finished, I made my way up to my living quarters. I was in no mood for my curious room-mate and his questions as he started up again. He told me that everyone had been sent home early, and he had tried to get into the mortuary but had found it locked from inside. He asked me where I'd been, and if I had been in the mortuary. I thought it best to ignore the questions, as I was acutely aware by this stage that this funeral was going to be different. He then asked me about my date. I told him I was tired and hadn't got to meet the girl at all as I'd had to work. I headed off to bed before he had a chance to ask me more.

AFTER COLLEGE the next day, we were all on duty. There was a total of three wakes on, but the funeral home had capacity for up to six at any one time, so in theory at least three wakes at once was no big deal. I was fascinated by this. We were all sent to different positions around the funeral home foyer and viewing areas. I was assigned to the office, where I had to deal with general queries and direct people to the right wake, though I was told to abandon my station if given the nod. There would be people coming in to hang up their coats and I wasn't to ask any questions. I had strict instructions to say very little and not to ask anything of them at all. I was also told that I would be attending to the needs of the family of the man I had brought from the airport, if they needed any help.

As the evening went on, I learned of the furore that had begun earlier in the day. The arrangements had all had to be changed at the last minute and, especially considering that the death notice had already been published, this was a huge problem to overcome.

Apparently, at that time, the Roman Catholic Archdiocese of Chicago had started to deny a public church funeral to persons with links to organised crime. So because of his associations with the mob, this man was not allowed into the basilica named in the obituary notice, which had been published that day. His family were very upset and were protesting, arguing bitterly that he had paid for the windows in that same church. The church had taken the booking when the funeral home staff were making the arrangements, but subsequently discovered that the deceased was Joe 'Caesar' DiVarco, and under no circumstances could he be allowed into the basilica under the ruling of the archdiocese. The bereaved were left with no choice but to have a wake for him in the funeral home on Tuesday and Wednesday evening. The removal would take place from the funeral home on Thursday morning, and the deceased would be taken to the mausoleum, where a funeral ritual would take place prior to the entombment. A deacon had agreed to officiate at this ceremony.

The arrangements were finally accepted, just in time to get the updated obituary notice published in the next day's issue of the newspaper. But the funeral home staff were very wary of what might happen in the course of the evening in the event of any altercation.

Ginny was working throughout the wake and she introduced me to the family, telling them that I would be looking after them if they needed anything. It was normal practice in the funeral home to introduce the staff on duty to the families. She was really angry with the archdiocese and clearly empathised with the family.

A priest came in to say prayers for one of the other wakes that evening. A relative of Joe DiVarco's happened to see him as he passed down the corridor. Some of the family spotted him and asked me to ask him to say the Rosary for Joe when he had finished the prayers at the other wake. I dutifully asked him, but I got a blank refusal. A little later, he was asked again by a family member and was clearly torn. Some other family members asked him, too, and were clearly angry. He was compelled by the decision of the archdiocese, and simply had no choice but to decline. He somehow managed to excuse himself from the situation and exit the building discreetly.

Throughout the evening, staff members subtly gestured to each other as many well-known mobsters entered the funeral home to pay their respects. These guys were immaculately dressed. If I'd met them on the street, I would have taken them for respectable, hardworking members of society. Of course, I had no idea who any of them were, though this seemed bizarre to all the other staff members. Two of these men had come from New York and were received with great respect. There were others who were definitely hanging around the funeral home in an extra-vigilant fashion. I was tipped off by staff members that there were FBI personnel coming and going too. I don't know how they knew one from the other! Tensions were high that evening with all that had happened that day.

My room-mate showed extra interest in every person that came to that wake, even though he was assigned to a different one. At one stage, I returned to the office to find him having a quick snoop around. I told him we were all supposed to do the jobs we had been assigned to. He asked me to tell him if anyone of interest came in. How was I going to do that, when I didn't even know the infamous man I had brought from the airport?! I sent him back to the wake he was attending to and told him again that we all had to do our own jobs there, especially that evening.

At one stage, I went out to check the car park and discovered that there were crews from TV news channels starting to gather to report on the funeral. They had big vans with satellite dishes and lights. There were reporters standing in front of the cameras. It was unbelievable to be in the middle of this, but I had to return to my post in the office.

Thankfully, the first repose for this man passed without any trouble but we still had the following evening to go.

I learned that huge efforts were often made to keep the funerals of these mobsters out of the media. There were also fears that the remains of deceased mobsters would be taken by rival gangs and a ransom would be demanded. The grieving family would have extra trauma to deal with should that happen. Staff told me that mobsters attending the funerals were also likely to be armed and wouldn't hesitate to use their weapons if the need arose.

Perhaps I had been sent to the airport for this man simply because I had no idea of who he was, and this would ensure that there was no leak of information about the funeral. To me, he was simply another person to be cared for.

The next day at college was like an inquisition. Fellow students had clippings, old and recent, with pictures of mobsters, including one of Joe 'Caesar' DiVarco. One of the students working at the funeral home was filling them in on who he had seen coming to the home, and how they tried to avoid getting photographed or questioned by the press outside. The other students were all familiar with these men from many reports in the media, and knew about their crimes and prison sentences.

I looked at the clippings as curious students asked me about the wake. I was horrified as I read about some of the heinous crimes committed by some of these mobsters. I instantly recognised a few of them in the photos – they were the noticeably well-dressed men I had observed at the wake. Many had already served long jail sentences. I found it hard to understand the crimes committed by these men, who somehow had led dual lives. They apparently had devoted and loving families in their lives, were active in their communities and yet managed to keep this all separate to their criminal activities. I had witnessed their true grief first hand in the funeral home. How could human beings have the appearance of love and kindness with one group of people, and then be able to inflict such pain on others in the course of their crimes? I will never be able to comprehend that.

On Wednesday after college, we returned to our stations in the funeral home as the wake continued for a second evening. Things were much the same, and thankfully the family was afforded respect as they grieved their loss, albeit of a man who had a lot to account for.

The next evening, Ginny continued her work as normal. She didn't thank me for my input over the previous four days, but then I wasn't used to thanks from her. It wasn't her way. She had clearly been holding back her emotions throughout the funeral, and this made me realise how truly professional she was in her work. Anyone else might have had an outburst of anger, or broken down in tears, but instead she channelled her energy into helping the family and keeping things calm for them. She also showed equal respect towards the other two families who had wakes there at the same time, to ensure that their grief wasn't overshadowed in any way by the drama surrounding Joe DiVarco's funeral.

I wasn't just learning about the preparation of the deceased, I was learning about respecting the bereaved and attending to their individual needs throughout the whole process.

Later that night, my room-mate was quizzing me again. He was on about the police patrol wagons ('squadrols') that brought people who had died suddenly to funeral homes. I had to get him to explain to me what he was talking about, as I had no notion. He told me that when a person died suddenly, the police working on squadrols were called. They then took the deceased to a nearby funeral home. However, once a deceased person was taken to a funeral home, the next of kin generally used the services of that funeral home. Even if the next of kin then chose a different funeral home, the first funeral home would bill the second funeral home for their services. Therefore, it was in the interests of funeral homes to have deceased persons brought to their premises by the police.

It was suspected that a practice had started whereby a small number of policemen were taking bribes from some funeral homes to choose them when they had a sudden death call. This was a totally illegal practice and would entail severe penalties for these members of the police force if it were uncovered. I could never have imagined such a thing being possible. The police whom I had met through my friend were good people. And indeed they were disgusted when, some time later, it came to light that this was in fact going on. The members of the force and the funeral directors involved were later caught, fined heavily and got varying suspended sentences. Some even got jail sentences.

Many, many years later, I had a visit from my room-mate. I didn't know what to expect from the visit, as we hadn't had what you could call a true friendship. We were work colleagues. We talked about our time in the funeral home way back then. He hadn't lost his curiosity for sure. During the course of the visit, he divulged that he had been working under cover for the government and had been wearing a wire at all times. He had been assigned to the funeral home to try to gain intelligence in relation to the 'Outfit'. With mobsters regularly attending funerals there, he had a good chance of getting information. When I met him, he described how uncomfortable it was wearing a wire, and having to conceal it from me. At that time, it was suspected that caskets were used for trafficking all kinds of goods. He also told me about the investigations into those members of the police force who had been bribed to take deceased persons to certain funeral homes. He said that it became big news when the culprits were found out and it hit the headlines.

I guess with the amount of extra time I was spending in the mortuary, he thought that, surely, I would have encountered some kind of funny business with caskets. Unfortunately for him, I hadn't the faintest clue what he was talking about when he had quizzed me about it.

Talking to him so many years later, it all made sense. He wasn't the strange guy that I thought he was, after all. He had been doing a really dangerous job at that time. He also told me that he regretted missing family time, as the work had entailed months on end working undercover with no contact with home in case phones were tapped by criminal gangs. It also explained his complete lack of experience with the deceased, despite the story about his uncle having a funeral home. He confessed how he'd really hated being around deceased persons, and that he'd had no idea of what to do. He had no interest in the course, which explained why he often nodded off in class. One day, an angry lecturer threw chalk at him to wake him up and reprimanded him. I had felt sorry for him that day, thinking he was exhausted from the work. I had no idea that his reason for being there had nothing to do with learning how to be a funeral director or embalmer. Ironic, when you think that I had travelled such a long distance from home to do the same course and work in the same job.

Cook County Morgue

THE FIRST DAY that I went to Cook County morgue was an eye opener for me, to say the least. I had gone to collect a deceased person with the other funeral directors from the funeral home.

The place was huge, and I never could have conceived of so many deceased persons in one building, and so many hearses coming and going in a totally organised fashion. Medical examiners and their pathologists examined up to 5,000 questionable deaths per year there. It was a very busy place. Once the paperwork was all in order, the deceased person would be released to the funeral director employed to look after the funeral. You would meet funeral directors from all over the city as they collected the deceased they were to look after.

What shocked me more was when I realised that there was a whole section where the unclaimed bodies of deceased persons were held. I couldn't comprehend how anyone could either die alone, ironically surrounded by people in a big city, and have no known next of kin, or have next of kin who simply didn't want to pick up the tab for a funeral for a relative from whom they were estranged, for whatever reason. That concept was completely alien to me, coming from Ireland. I had known of people who had no relatives left alive, but in those cases the community looked after them with fondness, and always gave them a good send-off. When someone died at home, the whole village stood still and the deceased was given total respect, with shops closing as the funeral cortège passed by.

I remember wondering what these individuals abandoned in Cook County morgue were like in life. Had they fallen on hard times? Had their own actions led them into this situation or had abuse by another stripped them of self-esteem and confidence? It was a really sad place to be, and showed in stark relief that not everyone gets the same chances in life or death.

One day, I was asked by one of the funeral directors if I would like to go with him and another colleague to Cook County morgue to collect a deceased person. As usual, I was really enthusiastic. I had been there a few times at this stage, so I expected us to be collecting a deceased person where the cause of death had been established by the medical examiner.

When we arrived, I automatically went to get the stretcher from the back of the ambulance. I was puzzled to discover that the ambulance held a completely different type of coffin. When I asked the funeral director about it, he explained that it was a steel coffin called a Ziegler case, a hermetically sealed casket. It could be used when there was a high risk of infection, if a person had died of a highly contagious disease. In this case, a see-through body bag could be used to seal the remains, making it possible for the bereaved to view the deceased. It was also possible to dress this type of coffin if it needed to be opened for the bereaved. It could also be used if the deceased had been dead for quite a long period of time.

When I had accompanied funeral directors to the morgue on previous occasions, they usually took the stretcher to the main mortuary and were met with the technicians working there, who helped them to transfer the deceased to the stretcher or casket. However, on this occasion, the technicians took the Ziegler coffin along a corridor on a trolley. My instinct was to follow, presuming that they were headed to another cold room area there. My funeral director colleagues immediately pulled me back and said that I wouldn't want to be following the technicians that day. I asked why, and was told discreetly that the person we were collecting had been dead for some time and was in a different area to where I had been before – they said the technicians were going to the 'rosy' room. It took me a minute to figure out what he meant. The rosy room was his satirical description of a room that had no smell of roses in it for sure!

They prepared me for what was to come by telling me that the person was badly decomposed. Past experience had taught them not to enter that particular cold room, as there was a very strong smell of death in there that was hard to escape even long after leaving the premises. But despite all of this discouragement, I still wanted to see the cold room for myself. The other two looked at each other in disbelief. I followed the technicians, who gave me a pair of black gloves, a mask and a full-size apron to put on.

I found it sad to see around fifteen deceased persons stored in large pull-out drawers in refrigerated units. These people would have been very difficult to identify. Even though I was wearing a pretty sturdy mask, the odour was nauseating and repulsive.

The poor deceased person we were collecting had been recovered from Lake Michigan after more than two months in the water. The technicians transferred the deceased person into two body bags before transferring him into the Ziegler coffin, which was to be sealed and not reopened, at the request of the family. I helped when I could, but stayed very much in the background, as I think my whole being was in a state of shock that day.

We left the cold room, removed the aprons, gloves and masks, and placed them in the dedicated bin. But as we wheeled the casket back to where the funeral directors waited, I could still smell the odour. It was either still in my nostrils, or it was on my hair and clothes.

My colleagues didn't hesitate to tell me that they could smell me coming, and they were reluctant to get into the ambulance with me. They asked if I wanted to go back in there to help two other funeral directors who were also collecting someone from the 'rosy' room. I declined, having had enough of the place for that day. I couldn't wait to get into the shower when we got back to the funeral home.

All that evening, I couldn't stop thinking about the bereaved of the deceased persons I had seen that day. Many of the deceased had gone well past recognition. Thanks to DNA developments in forensic science, the bereaved were at least able to be sure that they had the right person. Dental records also helped in this respect. So some would have the blessing of closure following the disappearance of a loved one, or once-loved one, even if they could never again see the person's face looking as it had in life.

I wondered about the man we had collected. Had he died accidentally, as a consequence of violence or from a decision to put an end to the pain of depression?

As it turned out, he'd left behind a family who were bereft. Apparently, he had gone missing after a boating accident with his sons. While they had managed to stay with the boat and were rescued, their father had not. The sons had walked the lakeshore tirelessly in the hope of finding his remains. Fortunately for them, he had been located by others, sparing them from seeing the badly decomposed remains of their beloved dad – although for those involved, it still would have been a pretty traumatic find. I will never forget the sadness at that funeral, combined with the family's sense of relief at finally laying their father to rest.

It made me think of bereaved people who are denied that closure through loss in tragic circumstances. Unfortunately, none of us can say for definite that we will be able to avoid such a terrible situation.

I had come to understand that funerals in America are really expensive, especially in densely populated cities like Chicago. Some faced the harsh reality of not being able to afford a funeral. This was the reason that some poor souls, despite being truly grieved, had to await burial or cremation along with other unclaimed bodies in Cook County morgue until such time as funds were mustered up. Sometimes this took several months.

Some of the souls in the morgue hadn't any form of identification, having had no fixed abode. When this happened, there was very little that could be done by the authorities, apart from waiting for a set duration of time, after which the city council would fund a basic burial (or nowadays, cremation).

While many people struggled to pay the costs of even a simple funeral, most people wanted to give their loved ones a good send off. In general, at the funerals I looked after, no expense was spared. I often saw beautiful and very expensive floral arrangements dumped after the funeral ceremony was over. This was mainly because there were strict rules in cemeteries with regard to what could and could not be placed on a grave plot. If a person was cremated, then the flowers were no longer needed. On a rare occasion, a family might take home the floral arrangement, but for most people, the idea of a casket spray of flowers on the coffee table in the living room didn't sit well. I suppose in that instance, the flowers, though pretty, were a painful reminder of the funeral.

When the time finally came for us to go to Cook County morgue as part of our practical studies in college, I was already familiar with it from my trips from the funeral home. On our first day there as a class, we were divided into groups of five or six. We had been studying the theory of embalming, and now it was time to put our knowledge into practice.

For once, I was ahead of my classmates, as I had come to America with a qualification. I was there to improve my skills and gain diverse experience. Many of my classmates were embalming for the first time, as the strict licensing laws and union policy in the States meant that, as students, they had only been allowed to assist with embalming. However, the college had an arrangement with Cook County morgue whereby unclaimed deceased persons would be embalmed by students under supervision, in a respectful way. This did not cost the state anything, as all services were being provided free of charge by the college.

I had expected to gain experience in working with all kinds of deceased persons, who had died in lots of different ways. However, it was like taking a step backwards for me. Our group was assigned to a deceased person, and we were individually tasked with different parts of the embalming and preparation process. My first assignment was to clip the toenails of the person we were looking after. I patiently stood and watched as the teacher explained how to embalm, and we all had our turn to participate. It was frustrating for me, as I didn't learn anything new that day. I watched some of my fellow students awkwardly learn to suture, or stitch the skin, which can be necessary for a few different reasons in the process of embalming. After an autopsy, the deceased is stitched by the pathologist. The embalmer then has to undo these stitches in order to inject the embalming fluid throughout the body. When the embalmer finishes, the deceased needs to be stitched once again. In this class, I was an A student.

After a few visits to the morgue with my class, I decided I should talk to my lecturer. I wanted to spend more time studying the other parts of the course curriculum in more depth. It was quite the turnaround, as I had really developed an interest in subjects that I had considered dropping only a few weeks prior to that.

I had a long discussion with him, and he agreed that I was ahead of my fellow students in the practical part of the course, partly thanks to my excellent mentors in the funeral home, whose standard was top class. Even though the prospect of going to Cook County morgue had been an initial draw to the course for me, I now found I was delighted to be able to spend time on other subjects on days when the rest of the class was there. I was really loving the course and wanted to learn as much as I could while I had the chance. I knew that whenever I decided to go home to Ireland, all of this information would be far harder to access. There were no books on death care or working with the deceased. There were no reference books for the embalmer to consult if they encountered difficult cases. Nowadays, the worldwide web has changed all that, thankfully, and much more is written on the topic now too.

As time went by, I was trusted to do more tasks at the funeral home on my own, getting experience in funeral directing from start to finish. One regular task assigned to me involved collecting the deceased from their place of death to bring them to the funeral home. This was usually quite straightforward, as I had become used to the roads and traffic in Chicago. However, on one occasion, the journey back with the deceased became somewhat less run-of-the-mill.

As I drove across a junction with a deceased person in the back of the ambulance, a car ran a red light and crashed straight into the side. There was great drama, as the mildly wounded people in the other vehicle moaned and screamed for help. Paramedics quickly arrived on the scene and began attending to the injured. Nobody needed hospitalisation. One of the paramedics then turned to me and asked me how I was. I said I was fine apart from a few scratches. I had overturned a car on my twenty-first birthday in Easkey – and was very lucky that nobody was injured in the accident – so, by comparison, this accident in Chicago was a really minor event.

The paramedic then asked if I had anyone else with me. I innocently replied that I had one person in my vehicle. She panicked and asked me how that person was. I calmly replied that she was dead. She asked to see them, I presume in the hopes of reviving them. She got very cross with me when she discovered that my passenger hadn't died as a result of the accident, but it had been her who had made the assumption. She thought I was mocking her, making fun of her work and wasting her time. It bothered me that she would think I would consider doing such a thing.

On my return to the funeral home, I had to report the accident to my boss. I was worried that I would have to pay for the repair to the ambulance or, worse still, that I would lose the trust they had put in me. They were concerned about the deceased person, but when they found out she hadn't sustained any bumps in the accident, they were relieved. They were also glad that I hadn't been hurt, and told me not to worry about the van, as insurance would cover that.

When I left the office, I told the others about my eventful afternoon. They thought it was funny when I told them about the paramedic. It was only then that I could see the funny side. I was lucky that I had not been badly hurt, nor caused harm to anyone else.

As time went on, my growing experience in the funeral home taught me how many different things could be involved when working with the deceased, some of which had never occurred to me before. For example, I'd never envisaged being involved with exhuming human remains. For me, when a deceased person went underground, that was their final resting place. But was different in the United States, where no task was too great or too unusual to be considered worth doing. That included exhumation.

There are many reasons, it turned out, why you may wish to remove a deceased person from the ground after burial. Sometimes it can be for public health reasons. It can also be necessary if a cemetery has to be relocated for any reason. In addition, a criminal investigation may call for human remains to be exhumed, or the bereaved may wish to move the deceased to a different location for personal reasons.

I have since been involved in many exhumations, but my first experience of it was in Chicago.

The process of exhumation is – perhaps unsurprisingly – not straightforward. No matter the reason for doing it, it is necessary to have a licence from the authorities as well as personnel from the appropriate authority present. Everything has to be checked in detail before the exhumation can take place. Serious errors could entail a lot of pain and hurt if the wrong grave is interfered with by mistake.

The area needs to be cordoned off and, depending on the location, it may be necessary to set up screens around the burial area to protect the privacy of all of the deceased buried in the plot. In my experience, work begins as early as possible in the day, as this is usually a quieter time, giving more privacy and also allowing for more daylight hours should the work take longer than expected due to unforeseen issues that may arise.

The man who was requesting the exhumation was the husband of the deceased lady. He often visited her grave and, ten years after her death, still missed her terribly. He had recently retired and was planning to move to California. He wanted to have his beloved wife reinterred in a cemetery near his new home so he could still visit her, and had gone through all the necessary paperwork. I was to be part of the team from the funeral home that was to look after the exhumation.

He was adamant that he wanted to see her again after all that time. This was a little unusual, but not out of the question.

We arrived at the cemetery early in the morning. The cemetery workers had done all the preparatory work. In

America, most cemeteries require that a vault is put in the ground to stop subsidence. It also ensures a solid foundation for the headstone or marker. The vault is delivered by a company and is dropped in the ground with a crane. After the casket is placed in it, a concrete lid with sealer ensures that the vault is sealed so it is airtight and watertight. So the casket we had to lift had been in a dry vault for ten years. I also noted from the paperwork that the casket was hermetically sealed, as is typical for expensive caskets. This meant the casket was also airtight.

At this stage, none of us could have had any idea of what we would see on opening the casket.

Two men from the state body were there, together with the widower and our team. After the casket was raised from the ground, it was taken to a building in the cemetery where it would be opened in private. Meanwhile, the widower was taken to the cemetery office. We would look at the remains first and then ask the widower again if he still wanted to see his late wife.

We set to work opening the casket. Normally, these caskets are opened with a special key, which turns a steel rod, which in turn moves and releases the two half lids, which are hinged on the opposite side of the casket. The casket was in amazing condition, despite having been underground for ten years. It wasn't as shiny as it would have been, but apart from that it looked fine. So we inserted the key expecting there to be a little resistance, but instead it was seized completely and would not budge. We tried and tried with no success. We didn't want to force it open. I was given the task of going to the office to inform the widower that we were having great difficulty in getting the casket open.

I could see the devastation in his face. His hands were shaking as he produced a folder of documents from the funeral directors who had buried his wife ten years earlier. The papers revealed that it was a top-of-the-range casket, eighteen-gauge, hermetically sealed – with guarantee! I guess you never know when you are going to need that guarantee.

The widower was still adamant that he wanted to see his wife.

I sat down with him and we chatted for a while. He explained to me that it was really, really important for him to see his wife again. I explained that he needed to be prepared for the fact that it was unlikely she would look the same as she had in the casket at the time of the funeral. He argued that the funeral directors that had looked after his wife's funeral had assured him that she was embalmed and that she would be preserved because of the process. It was difficult, but I had to explain to him that embalming wouldn't preserve his wife forever, but that the process delayed the decomposition process. He was clearly upset by this revelation, but was still determined to proceed with opening the casket. I warned him that it may cause irreparable damage to the casket, entailing the purchase of a new one. We both laughed when he mentioned the guarantee and the possibility of looking for a replacement casket due to a faulty locking system.

I also asked him if I could let him know of the condition of his late wife's body if we succeeded in opening the casket by force. Then he could at least prepare himself for what he was about to see. I then went back over to the building where the casket was and told the others that the man still wanted to have the casket opened.

After a lot of effort and force, we finally opened it. I couldn't believe what lay before us in the casket. There was a fog of white fibre over the face and down over the body of the lady. I began to move the fibre gently away to reveal what lay underneath, but was stopped by one of the senior funeral directors. He told me not to touch it for a minute as he took a closer look. He then turned to me and revealed that it was the lady's hair.

I had not thought that this was possible. I looked closer and realised that it was. I have since asked several experts about this, but nobody can explain this hair growth after death. It most certainly wasn't normal.

We brought the man to see his late wife. He was a bit shocked by what he saw, but I realised that seeing her had, at the same time, brought him a great sense of relief. She wasn't as he had expected to see her, but what was important to him was that he did get to see her, in the outfit she had been laid to rest in, though now looking much too big for her. She was transferred to another casket and arrangements were made for burial in her final resting place down in California.

I never witnessed anything like this again and cannot explain what I saw. The woman's husband verified that her hair was certainly not as long as that when she died. It was bizarre.

Ireland or America?

DEATH CALLS IN MANY different ways. You never know when, or from where, you might have to collect a deceased person. When I say each death is different, I mean just that.

I can usually remember each of the different circumstances when I have had to collect a deceased person from their place of death when they have not died at home or in hospital. Why can I remember these episodes so vividly? I don't have any scientific way of answering this, but in my view, it must have something to do with my brain being on extreme alert when attending these scenes. It's as if they are stored in a special place in my mind. I can usually tell from the initial phone call that something really difficult lies ahead.

When I get a call to any of these unusual circumstances, my whole self goes into overdrive as I travel to the place where I have to go. I suppose my subconscious is preparing me for the trauma that may lie ahead. In my mind, I try to ready myself for all possible eventualities. In reality, this is next to impossible, of course, as one cannot predict the circumstances exactly until you reach the place where the deceased person is. I know I may have to face something very traumatic, but I will never have any idea of how I will be affected emotionally by what lies ahead.

I ask myself what equipment I might need. Will I need extra help in terms of people power, or even the assistance of a machine, to enable me to bring that person away from their place of death?

It often takes me many days to process the whole thing, but in my work, I cannot stop to look after my own needs. I have to keep going as I look after the needs of others who have to get through a funeral or funerals of dearly loved persons. Maybe this involvement in itself is what helps me to cope.

There is such tremendous sorrow and shock at these times for everyone involved.

One of the first such tragedies that I encountered was during my time in America in the coldest days of winter. I got a call from the police to attend a scene where two people had been found dead in a car and needed to be taken for an autopsy. I had presumed that there had been some kind of car crash, but I had no idea of what I would find when I arrived.

Heavy snow showers were not uncommon in the depths of winter, and vast amounts of snow could fall in a very short space of time. It turned out that one such fall of snow was responsible for the deaths of two fine young people. The young man had just got his driving licence and was very proud of his first car. He had called to collect his girlfriend to take her out for a meal on her birthday.

They had obviously delayed for a cuddle, possibly while waiting for a break in the snow shower. It was so cold that they had probably had the car running in order to keep warm. The car was still running when the police came.

The snow had come down heavily, very quickly, and had obstructed the exhaust pipe. It was an older car and fumes from the exhaust had filled the car. The couple died cuddled together, having fallen asleep from carbon monoxide poisoning. What was even more tragic was the fact that the girl's family were right inside her home watching TV, and they had no idea that their lovely daughter had died on their front driveway, never to return from her birthday date alive.

How could both of these families ever get over the pain of such a tragic loss? Two happy, healthy teenagers, wiped out by an unexpected twist of fate, falling asleep together never to wake up, having breathed poisonous fumes that quickly claimed their lives.

Another time, I was called to an apartment where a friend had accidentally shot her best friend with the friend's own gun.

Her best friend was being badly abused by her boy-friend. She had ended the relationship with him, but he was still threatening her. She had been advised to buy a gun for her own safety and protection by her friend and others. She did this reluctantly. But she dreaded the return of her ex-boyfriend and had decided to keep the gun hidden under her couch in the living room so that she would have easy access to it should he ever break into the apartment. She wasn't accustomed to guns and unfortunately had hidden that gun loaded with bullets.

When her friend called over to visit, she told her about the gun that she had purchased to protect herself in case her ex-boyfriend ever came to attack her. Her friend was surprised that she had got a gun, but thought it to be a good plan in light of the violence her friend had encountered at the hands of her ex-boyfriend.

She carefully took out the gun to show her friend and handed it to her to hold. Her friend knew little more than she did about guns. She took the gun and held it, and, as she surveyed it, she pulled the trigger. She had no idea that the gun was loaded, so she was shocked when instead of a click came the loud gunshot. She was devastated when she realised that she had just shot her best friend dead.

The irony of this was that both thought it was a good idea for this woman to have a gun to protect herself. Little did either of them know that rather than protecting her, that gun would instead take her life.

I remember attending the scene when the police had established what had happened. It was clear that the death was a complete accident. But I will never forget seeing the friend totally inconsolable outside the building. She was distraught by what had just happened. Not only had she lost her best friend, but she was the one who had pulled the trigger.

The dead woman's family were also inconsolable. They kept thinking that had she not met that boyfriend in the first place, none of this would ever have happened. They knew that the gun should not have been loaded. Fingerprints proved that it had been loaded by their lovely daughter and her sister, and that her friend had had nothing to do with that. However, they were very bitter at how she was shot at close range. They blamed the friend for being stupid, thinking she should have checked first and ensured that the gun wasn't loaded. They couldn't believe that she would point a gun, loaded or otherwise, at someone. These were all things that unfortunately can never be undone.

It was such a sad and tragic scene to be called to. I often shudder when I see any kind of gun and know the terrible pain and loss that it is capable of inflicting. Of course, handguns, like the one that shot this woman, are readily available for purchase in America, and sadly we have seen far too many such accidents over the years.

Seeing the victims of gunshot wounds was not uncommon when I was working in Chicago. The company I worked for had many branches around the city and so looked after funerals of different communities. This inevitably also included those of gang members. But you had to remember that they too had families grieving them.

I ended up embalming a gang leader, and subsequently ended up supervising the wake of the same man. His family came in as mourners usually did, and the visitation went as normal. I was working between the office and the foyer. I was on my own as my colleague was not able to work that evening and had asked me to cover for him.

Things were quiet enough, and I figured that I might even get home early. Then something unusual happened. The family all left the visitation room a lot earlier than expected. I wasn't sure if they were all gone or if they were coming back, so I waited and wondered. But then I noticed that four men had come in wearing black. They went into the visitation room. I was about to follow them in to tell them that the family were gone and that they had missed them. However, I was stopped abruptly in my tracks when I heard an almighty bang. I was terrified. I figured that it could well have been a shot that had been fired. I did not know what to expect next. I retreated to the office and locked the door, then crouched down under the desk, bringing the phone with me. I dialled the company manager's number, and every number seemed to make so much noise! I asked him to call the police for me and to send help. I was sure I was going to be shot before they left the building.

As I spoke to the manager, he told me to calm down. He asked me if my colleague had filled me in on this funeral. I had no idea what he was talking about and, in my defensive position under the office desk, I wasn't able to listen properly to what he was saying, as I was listening intently to see if the men were coming my way. At some point, I must have put the phone down.

I heard footsteps coming out of the repose room. My heart pounded as I wondered what would happen next. Then, I heard the front door open and close. I thought I'd heard the men leave the building but I wasn't sure. I waited in silence, wondering if I was alone and if it was safe to investigate. After what seemed like ages, but was probably only a few minutes, I plucked up the courage to leave the office. I quietly moved towards the repose room and cautiously peered in, expecting to find someone dead on a chair or on the floor. I was puzzled to see nobody there.

I looked at the floor for any sign of blood or evidence of a shooting, but all looked normal.

I began to wonder if I had been mistaken; perhaps the bang had only been something falling or simply a door banging.

I had put a lot of effort into ensuring that the deceased person looked well in the casket prior to the wake, so I did what was normal for me – I approached the casket to check that he still looked alright after the viewing. What lay before me was shocking. To my horror, I saw that the deceased man had been shot in the head. What was this all about, I asked myself. Why would anyone do such a thing?

I called the manager again, and this time I listened properly to what he had to say. Apparently, it had become a practice for this particular gang to shoot all deceased members in the head after their families had viewed them and had said their final goodbyes. They believed it would ensure that the members – or, in this case, the leader – could not bring the secrets of the gang with them in death.

It sounds very bizarre, and makes no logical sense to the ordinary citizen, but for this group in the midst of gang warfare, they were taking no chances, even after death!

DESPITE THE SAD and sometimes shocking things I encountered in the course of my work in this big American city, which was so different to what I had been used to growing up in the West of Ireland, things couldn't have been going better for me in my life at that time. I had a really good job in Chicago, in a funeral home I loved, working alongside really nice people. I had great friends whom I had met through my course and through the Irish community in Chicago. I had even been offered a job at another funeral home owned by the company, with better accommodation and pay, and more responsibility. It was an honour for me to be promoted.

So would I stay? At that time, staying on in America was looking like a very attractive option for me, as my career was really taking off there. But I was torn. I still had a strong desire to return to Ireland and set up my own business, but at the same time, on many occasions I was very tempted to settle in Chicago.

Then one day, the company told me that I needed to take some time off as I had holidays accumulated. The months had flown by so fast and I had been enjoying the work so much that I hadn't even thought to take any time off, and now almost a month was due to me. I decided to take a two-week trip home to Ireland. As well as affording me the chance to catch up with friends and family, I was hoping that the visit would help me to decide whether to return home permanently and pursue my original dream or carry on living in Chicago.

I arrived home to find that not a lot had changed in Easkey, except for more businesses closing down. There was still a huge amount of emigration and it was affecting the economy in a bad way.

While I was at home, I made contact with Val O'Connor. It was lovely to talk to him again. He was delighted to hear about all my experiences in Chicago. He invited me to Cork to see everyone again, and of course I accepted the invitation willingly. While I was there, I spent some time in the mortuary with the other embalmers, whom I had got on well with when I was working there. I shared some of the knowledge that I had gained and Val was impressed. He asked me if I would stay for a week to share skills and tips, and I was pleased to do so. I recognised my own passion for death care in a young man called Vivan O'Sullivan, who had been trained as an embalmer for the funeral home after I left Cork to go to America. Vivan was keen to learn more skills and eagerly took on board everything that I showed him. This enthusiasm for learning struck a chord with me and was possibly the spark for me developing an embalming course many years later.

As the week passed, I spent a lot of time with Val and we talked about many things. One day, on my return to the office after a funeral, there was a message for me to call my father. It was very unusual for him to call me. I phoned him, anxious that there was something wrong at home. To my relief, he was calling me to tell me that there was a site for sale in the centre of Ballina. Before I went to Chicago, I had identified this site as one that would be ideal for a funeral home if I ever got a chance to develop my own business. The public auction for the site was to take place the following day, and he was wondering if I was going to go to it. I told him that I wasn't.

The day after the auction, I contacted the auctioneers to see if the site had been sold. I discovered that it hadn't, as the highest bid had only been IR£35,000. I asked if they were still willing to sell it and if so, what price would secure the property. I was told that IR£65,000 would seal the deal. I was shocked at the low price, as this property had been for sale before I went to Chicago with a price tag of IR£150,000.

I promptly asked my father to put the IR£5,000 deposit on the site to secure the purchase. He lent me the money to buy it, on condition that I would pay him back in time. Over the years I kept my word and paid him back the money I owed him.

Funerals in rural Ireland hadn't changed since I went to Chicago. I wanted to make a difference now. For the most part, there weren't many full-time funeral directors. Funeral directing remained an add-on for many other types of businesses. Many didn't see any reason to invest anything in the business apart from updating the hearse from time to time.

I wanted to change all of this and bring the techniques and the dedicated professionalism I had learned in Chicago back to Ireland, to support our traditions and the respect paid as a matter of course to the bereaved and their families. It was a brave thing to embark on at the time. It was a new concept to be just a funeral director, and the idea of building a funeral home in rural Ireland seemed mad to many. However, I knew that there were many funeral directors in need of embalming services, and it was going to be possible for me to make a living through working as an embalmer throughout the region. This gave me a sense of security until I could eventually survive running my own funeral business in my custom-designed funeral home.

The general public was used to going to the residence of the deceased or, the other main alternative, the hospital mortuary. While the staff in these places were excellent, a hospital mortuary back then was a very clinical and cold place to be. There were very few funeral homes in Ireland at that time, and I was clear that I wanted the funeral home I was going to build to be among the best in the country in terms of scale and facilities.

Still, though, with interest rates at 18 per cent at the time, it was a very brave move. I had the energy and determination of youth on my side, and I saw the potential of it. I knew that once the public discovered that there was a better way of looking after the deceased, there would be no turning back. The early years would be the most difficult to get through, with a mortgage to be paid and a doubtful public to attend to. If I could get through these first years, then I was sure that I would lead the way for a new way of looking after the deceased in rural Ireland, without losing the traditions of the Irish funeral.

This site coming up to buy at such a good price was too good an opportunity to let it pass me by. I hadn't been sure what to do, but here was the realisation of my original dream coming true. Now I had to decide the best path forward. It was going to take quite a lot of money to build the funeral home I wanted. I was living a new and exciting dream in Chicago, so I could go back there and carry on, saving more money towards the development of the funeral home, or I could just begin the project straight away. I had worked hard in the time I was in Chicago and had not been foolish with my earnings, so I had money saved.

I had long conversations with Joe from the funeral home in America. He wanted me to come back to Chicago but understood my predicament. He said he would hold my job open for me for six months, which would give me time to make solid plans. This was generous and a real privilege. It enabled me to focus on the task at hand while knowing that I didn't have to sacrifice the job I was so happy in just yet as I explored my future prospects. He knew that I couldn't turn down an opportunity to set up my own business in Ireland, which had been my original plan, but he hoped I would return to work in Chicago.

I'd left Chicago without any real farewell, as it was always my intention to return after the two-week trip home. I really loved Chicago, but my love for Ireland was rekindled when I stepped back on Irish soil. When I went to visit the site after I had purchased it, I was able to visualise my funeral home and I knew that I had gained the confidence and expertise to make my dream a reality. I realised

I had to go all in with this opportunity that had been presented to me. I hadn't lived lavishly in America so I had pretty much all of my important stuff in that humble suitcase of mine when I came home. And so I made the decision. I never returned to work in Chicago after that.

To this day, though, I often open up that old suitcase of mine and reminisce on those happy days full of really good people.

Without delay, the papers were signed and the site was mine to develop. I found an architect to draw up plans for my funeral home. He patiently humoured me as I explored how my building would work for my style of carrying out funerals – bearing in mind, that this was a concept that existed only in my mind, and he was trying really hard to understand what I wanted! He made suggestions that were practical in general building terms and ensured that health and safety were attended to in detail. He also found ways of designing the building to suit my needs.

It was essential that it should have the feeling of a home. It was never to be a substitute for a church or a mortuary, rather something more domestic. It had to be possible to manage large crowds in the building, safely moving them through. I needed a grand entrance with a canopy and pillars. This would lead the visitor into a foyer to match any fancy hotel of the day with a welcoming fireplace. The foyer was to be a place where people could gather before and after sympathising with the bereaved. In the private office, people would be able to make funeral arrangements in comfort. I wanted to include two visitation rooms, one smaller to suit smaller gatherings and intimate prayer or secular services.

The mortuary had to be in a separate building close by, where the deceased could be embalmed and prepared for repose. Other funeral directors requiring my services as an embalmer would need to be able to come and go to this building without affecting funerals in my funeral home. I wanted to have the option to live upstairs, as I had lived over funeral homes in America. With the prospects of a hefty loan ahead, I wasn't going to be in any position to get a mortgage for a house as well any time soon. It made sense to be able to live on site.

A standby consideration for the building was the option to turn it into two houses, in the event of all plans going belly up. Fortunately, this option never had be explored.

I was successful in my application for planning permission, and then I had to navigate the world of getting a mortgage on a unique building, that was essentially a gamble for any bank to take on at the time. Fortunately, my father had always been a shrewd businessman, keeping his financial affairs in good order, and had earned the trust of the banks. With him as guarantor, I was eventually accepted for a mortgage. It was a challenging time for me as I navigated the world of building as well as the financial side of setting up a new business, but I was fortunate to have a team of really good craftsmen on board from start to finish.

By 1990, the funeral home was ready to open. Unlike a hotel or shop, there was no splash in the local press to announce my new business. People were wary of death and were not inclined to talk about it, let alone come and explore a new building purpose-built for funerals, so advertisements in the paper would have been considered in bad taste at the time.

I had faith in my concept, and I was confident in the skills I had learned in America. However, it was not guaranteed that the community would take to this notion of a funeral home when there weren't many in Ireland at the time. You put a huge amount of trust in someone when you allow them to look after a recently departed loved one. I was known by many in the region, of course, but still, I was opening a new business, in an area many people feel uncomfortable talking about, and trying to bring together the old ways of doing things with something more modern. Would it work? Would people be too sceptical of change?

Not long after I opened, I remember showing a group of friends around my funeral home. I could tell they had no understanding of my concept. It was the era of night clubs, when the general public was moving away from dances in halls. My friends knew that my business was quiet at that

time and, in an effort to keep me upbeat, they said that
you couldn't fail with the building, as it could always be
turned into a fine night club. My heart sank to hear this,
and I realised that I had a lot of convincing of the general
public ahead of me.

A Home in a Funeral Home

LITTLE BY LITTLE, more and more people began to use McGowan's Funeral Directors. I will never forget the first few funerals and the families that placed their trust in my services. Over time, I was able to marry the traditional wake in the house with the use of the funeral home, to enable families to have the intimacy of their own home for relations and close friends, and then the facility of the funeral home to cater for larger crowds coming to pay their respects. Though things have moved on in some respects from what I remember from my childhood, funerals in the West of Ireland are still a large affair, with vast numbers of people coming out to support the bereaved throughout the different stages of the funeral. I am glad that this community support is still common in rural Ireland.

Aside from the general uncertainty as to how people would take to the business, in the early days there were plenty of practical challenges too. In 1990, there were no mobile phones, and the landline was plugged in to the wall in one location in the building. Extra sockets came at a premium, so we had just two phones initially. These weren't cordless, so answering often involved a quick dash to get to the phone in time before it rang out. If you missed a call, there was no way of finding out who had called, unless they called again later. This was a disaster at a time when the main source of work came via the phone, as telecommunications were constantly improving in Ireland at that time.

I was able to divert the phones in the evening to the business in Easkey, where I was living at that time, but the problem came when I was travelling between the two, as I always had to make sure that someone was ready to answer. I was also working in the bar in Easkey in the very early days, and coordinating the two wasn't easy.

As I started to take on more work at the funeral home, however, it made sense to move into the modest apartment upstairs that I'd had put in when the building was constructed. It probably wouldn't be everyone's choice – to live in the place where they work, even if their job doesn't involve what mine does – but I was very happy to do this.

It was bare to begin with, to say the least! But it did me fine. My aunt and uncle gave me a portable black-and-white TV to kill the time at night. On colder evenings, before I got the heating connected upstairs and could afford money for extra oil, I used to close the kitchen door and use the oven to heat the small kitchen, turning it on briefly to heat up the space. I might add that the manager in a different bank in town was kind enough to give me a loan that enabled me to finish upstairs so that I could move in. This was at a time when my main mortgage bank would give me no leeway.

Life over the funeral home was busy, and I had good friends who called in, and brought life into my new home.

I was really tied to the building at that time, so when my phone company told me about the possibility of a pager, I was delighted. That meant that I could get a brief message on a pager that I could wear on my belt.

Cordless phones were the next major improvement for me. Imagine being able to walk across the road and still talk on the landline! That was so exciting and liberating for me. Hard to understand when you consider today's level of communications.

Around 1991, I invested in my first mobile phone. What a wonderful invention. Now I could take calls anywhere (pending signal) and be away from the building for up to two hours. That was the battery life of this large, cumbersome item that didn't fit in any pocket. For some at the time, a mobile phone was a symbol of prestige, but for me, it enabled me to have a taste of normal life, even if it was for a short period of time.

I started a wreath-making business, supplying funeral directors all over the country with artificial floral tributes for funerals. This business kept me busy on the 'quiet' days, while also keeping the wolf from the door. I had some part-time staff at this stage, who all mucked in making wreaths.

When I was young, before I went to Chicago and was working in our Spar supermarket, the bane of my life was a teenager with her hair in two plaits called Aileen Donagher. She would regularly swoop to a halt outside the shop and jump off her bike, tossing it towards the window. Many times, I was sure she would break the glass!

However, in the summer of 1990, I got to know her as an adult, and we fell madly in love. We married in June 1992, and my small apartment over the funeral home became our first family home.

We had lots of happy times there when our first two little girls, Mary and Bríd, came along. It was difficult for them to understand that they needed to keep quiet upstairs while a funeral was taking place downstairs. They met many different people at that time, who came into the funeral home for various reasons, some making funeral arrangements, some settling their accounts or just popping in for a visit. Things like safety stair gates were not an option for us, as the stairs to our apartment led down to the coffin display area. On the advice of a friend, the girls were taught how to slide down the stairs on their tummies, which they thoroughly enjoyed! Sometimes, they would sit at the top of the stairs and watch quietly as people attending a funeral passed by the bottom of the stairs.

One day, one of them toddled, with her soother in her mouth, up to the front of the main visitation room. She stood in front of the coffin and turned to face the grieving family. A family member lifted her up and brought her to me in the office, saying, 'I think this is yours!' in a friendly way. We both laughed and the toddler was swiftly brought back upstairs again.

It wasn't easy keeping two young children quiet upstairs, so Aileen often had to bring the girls out during removals and return just as we were driving out with the hearse. She had it down to a fine art, and they would watch from across the river as they sat in the car, arriving back just in time to lock up and turn off lights following a removal. It was then time to get the girls ready for bed.

We always talked openly to our children about death. They would regularly stand with us for a brief moment beside the coffin and say a little prayer for the deceased person and all of the 'sad' people who were grieving.

We were blessed with lovely babysitters at that time, too, though it wasn't always easy to get babysitters who weren't afraid to stay over a funeral home.

Lots of people used to look at us when we told them we lived over a funeral home. 'Are you not scared?' they would ask. We were never afraid in the funeral home. We lived with death, and, though it may sound odd, the deceased had a very strong and often comforting presence. We always showed respect for the deceased and brought our children up to do the same.

I suppose when you know many of the deceased who stayed with us downstairs, there wasn't any reason to be afraid!

One issue was that the children did not have a safe place to play on their little trikes in the funeral home grounds. It would have been quite dangerous, as cars, hearses and delivery vans were in and out regularly. Our girls were happy to cycle around the coffins in the coffin display room, learning quickly not to cycle too near the wooden corners, as they soon understood that a collision with a coffin corner was a painful affair, requiring a 'kiss it better' kiss from Mam or Dad, before getting up on the saddle again to resume play.

When the phone rang in the funeral home, it was a signal to everyone to be quiet for a few moments, until the identity of the caller was established. Noise could resume if it was a friend calling, but if it was a funeral call, respect had to be shown by keeping quiet.

Living over the funeral home often meant we were aware of people calling to the front door at all hours. People often called late at night to collect umbrellas or look for gloves etc. that they would have forgotten at some stage. Gerry, my father-in-law, couldn't understand why I could never sit down and finish a cup of coffee with him until one weekend he offered to cover for us when we went to a wedding in Cork. On our return, he attempted to make a cup of tea for us and the doorbell rang. He looked at us and laughed. 'It's been like this all weekend!' he said. 'I have boiled the kettle so many times and have not made one cup of tea!'

Life in general was like that in the funeral home. That doorbell was constantly ringing for all kinds of reasons.

When the weather was nice, the girls spent lots of time at Aileen's family home in Easkey, where Grandad Gerry, or 'GaGa', as they then called him, provided lots of entertainment, including a tree house and many adventures. We also had support from my family, and we were very lucky to have a brilliant childminder who was like a second mother to them. Our girls have lovely childhood memories, despite the fact that they were often shipped here and there as we responded to the increasing workload in the funeral home.

In 1997, we moved into our home on the outskirts of Ballina. As we emptied the cardboard boxes of our belongings, the girls quickly turned them into 'coffins' and began playing 'funerals' as they replicated a funeral cortège along the upstairs landing.

As the business developed, a day's work involved talking to many, many people about different things. There were days when it was really draining physically and emotionally. I have to admit that it was nice to have our new home to go to after work. Developing a new garden can be torture for many, but for me it gave me some headspace and time to think. There's something refreshing about the smell of freshly cut grass.

Our youngest daughter, Eithne, arrived two years after we moved into our home, so it was nice to be able to escape and have some family time whenever I had the chance, as I often had to miss out on family occasions when they clashed with a busy time in the funeral home.

When the TV series *Six Feet Under* came out a few years later, we loved the programme as it resonated immediately with life in the McGowan household prior to moving out of the funeral home. We were glued to the weekly episodes!

The Science of Death

IN IRELAND, our many traditions around death help us to cope with that final goodbye. Time spent reminiscing and grieving the loss in the period prior to the funeral ritual, and indeed afterwards, is very precious. So I consider it vital, in my roles as funeral director and embalmer, to ensure that the deceased person appears true to themselves as they lie among their loved ones for those final hours. In my work, I try to restore the appearance of the person, as far as is possible, to that of their living self. This is to ensure that the final visual memory of that much-loved person is as natural as possible. The last time you see someone is most likely to be one of your strongest memories of them in the years ahead.

Sometimes, death is hailed as a natural part of life itself and presents as a gentle passing, where everyone close gets to share very dear time together and say some sort of goodbye. However, I know of far too many people who have felt robbed of the opportunity to utter words of love before that final parting, as in the case of a sudden death or not being able to travel home in time to be there. Other people may be present but find themselves unable to utter those emotional words for no known reason. This is yet another reason why the wake, the ritual whereby we begin to say goodbye to someone we have lost, is so important, and why it's vital that the person who has died looks as they did in life.

In most cases, we are unprepared for the physical changes that occur after death. Some of these changes are accelerated by something as simple as a spell of warm weather. In winter, too, heating in a house where the person passed can contribute to the decomposition process. Other changes cannot be predicted, and sometimes can be attributed to the very cause of death itself.

It's something that many of us prefer not to think about; although, in the course of my work, I do get asked a lot of questions about death and what happens to our physical form when we die. So, in this section of the book, I will try to answer these questions. In general, the public knows very little about things like decomposition, embalming and cremation. I want to explain what happens and why good death care is important to deceased and bereaved alike. Because if we don't talk about things, we will always have a fear of them. I'll give you some scientific detail in plain English. If you don't want to know about this or will find this sort of information upsetting, please skip to the next chapter. If you have recently lost someone and you are not ready to hear about this just yet, you can always come back another time. I am sharing my experience not to sensationalise my work but rather to demystify both the natural processes that take place after death and the work of an embalmer and funeral director.

Many factors can change the features of a person after death. Sometimes, these changes can be distressing and frightening to experience, in terms of what is physically happening and the rapidity of change. When I was first working for my father's business, I didn't like the idea of telling a family that we would have to close the coffin, fumbling through excuses, without at least trying to be proactive by tackling the physical issues. That was a big reason why I wanted to learn more about what I could do to help, prompting me to study mortuary science. Death itself is traumatic enough, without the decomposition process taking its toll on the deceased.

Back in the early days of my embalming career, before I went to America, much of my work was carried out in houses, with no facilities for embalming. The wake continued in the room next door and silence befell the place any time I exited the room where I was working. They were very challenging circumstances for me to work in, and sometimes the expectations of me were nothing short of those of an alchemist. It was a lonely task, no internet to consult, no mobile phones to phone a friend, just me on my own, doing my best for the poor soul in my care.

Very often, the deceased might not have been released from a hospital until late in the evening. In the case of a person passing at home, if it was a busy flu season, understandably, the local doctor had to prioritise the living. My work could not begin until a doctor had certified the death. So for one reason or another, I often found myself working at night. This was often after finishing work in the bar, when I would get a call or a message and have to set off on my journey, alone with my thoughts, as I prepared myself for what might be ahead of me.

These journeys were lonely, with no Google maps, no mobile phones, just a piece of paper on the passenger seat with the directions to the house and a landline number to call, if there was one. Did I ever get lost? Yes! But back then, you just retraced your journey and tried alternative roads. If you were near a village, you could use the public telephone kiosk, if you had remembered to throw some change in the car to pay for the call. For the most part, though, many of the houses with a phone didn't actually have any service at nighttime.

The wake house was usually easy enough to identify, though, as it would be the only house lit up in the area, and there were usually a few people standing outside on the lookout, ready to assist me however they could. People were very good like that, and just wanted to help in any way in order to ease the burden for the bereaved. Following my work, I had to sit in my car and drive home. Sometimes I had the pleasure of experiencing the dawn on my way back, which is a special time of the day.

Nowadays, I always insist on bringing the deceased person to my own custom-designed mortuary, where I have all equipment and resources to hand, tailored to suit my needs as an embalmer. I have modelled my facility on surgical theatres, and have also taken notes from mortuaries in the USA and other countries around the world. But back then, I would turn up with my two black cases, often to find the deceased on the bed where they had passed, in a small bedroom, and I would have to do what I could. I'd close the door behind me, while the family retreated to another room, and peel back the sheet to reveal the task ahead. What would I need to do, to delay the inevitable changes that death would bring to this person's human body? It was a huge responsibility, placed on my shoulders in very rudimentary conditions.

The work I do is about more than the mere skill of presenting a person to perfection. It is, in essence, the connection that I make with the deceased person that guides my work and the approach I take. This, obviously, is easier when I knew the person in life. If I haven't had the privilege of knowing the person, I have to build a picture of that character through all the information that is presented to me. Photographs, stories, jewellery, shoes, even the chosen outfit, all tell me about this person. Sometimes, a special item that went everywhere in that person's pocket says it all.

I believe that I have received guidance from elsewhere, which has helped me to get it right on numerous occasions. I have on occasion got it wrong and, in my belief, I was checked, in no uncertain terms, from the other side!

The purpose of embalming is not to preserve the remains, but more to delay the decomposition process, to hold back the natural processes that would be distressing to the loved ones of the deceased as they say their goodbyes. In the course of my career, I have seen many changes in how embalming is practised. Nowadays, the process is more accurately called the hygienic treatment of the deceased. Even though the term 'embalming' really refers to the process carried out by the ancient Egyptians, who would spend two months mummifying the body to preserve it for the afterlife, it has stuck and is the most commonly used term among funeral professionals when referencing the hygienic treatment process.

When I first learned how to embalm, the only embalming fluid available contained a high strength of formaldehyde, which had the effect of making the remains quite hard and stiff to touch. In fact, one embalmer once told me that the best way to know that the process was complete was by pressing gently on the skin of the deceased – if it was hard, the person was well embalmed. I used to hate the smell that remained on my person, even after showering. This was actually the gaseous form of formaldehyde that had attached itself to me as I worked. Formaldehyde is also carcinogenic. After seeking alternatives, I moved away from high-strength formaldehyde to different chemicals that are much safer for embalmers to use.

The embalmer needs to dress appropriately for the process. A mask prevents them from inhaling anything potentially harmful, and goggles protect the eyes from accidental splashes, either of bodily fluids or embalming fluids. Gloves are a must. A long disposable gown, similar to that worn during surgical procedures, is usually worn over scrubs, for protection. As the embalmer is standing for the duration of his or her work, we must ensure we wear comfortable, waterproof footwear. A first-aid kit needs to be always at the ready, in case of any accidental cuts or splashes.

So, what, basically, does the process of embalming entail?

It involves injecting embalming fluid into the body, employing the vascular network, i.e. arteries and veins. There are key points on the body where the embalmer can confidently inject, and the most common one of these is the carotid artery in the neck. A small incision has to be carefully made in the skin, and then a further even smaller incision into the artery itself, just enough to enable the insertion of the embalming needle. The fluid enters the body through this needle. An embalming machine has a container holding the correct mix of embalming fluid and water, as well as a controlled pump, which allows the embalmer to control the pressure of fluid entering the vascular system.

When I first began the embalming process, there was no machine available here in Ireland to assist with the process. So when I went to a house, I used special jars, along with a hand-pump system. The system worked on the same principle as the pump in a garden sprayer, where you build up pressure by pumping up and down.

During the embalming process, the area where most care must be exercised is the head. This is done slowly and monitored carefully until the embalmer is confident that the head has been thoroughly embalmed. It is a miraculous experience to witness the way that areas such as the ears can come back to their natural colour. In many cases, the ears can become a blueish colour after death, especially when death has been from a cardiovascular problem. This is often referred to as livor mortis.

When the head is properly injected, fluid is then sent around the body until all areas have been reached. Where there has been a breakdown of a blood vessels, the embalmer may have to find a second or third site to inject into. If a post-mortem has been carried out, the vessels will have been severed in places.

When I first began to embalm under supervision, there are two things that I recall having great difficulty with. The first was actually making my first small incision. It was a combination of a fear of damaging a blood vessel with the thought of inflicting pain when cutting through a person's skin. Even though I knew the person was beyond feeling pain, this was, indeed, a hurdle I had to overcome in my mind.

I also found suturing – stitching – really difficult in my student days, for the same reason. I am sure that medical students will all empathise. At one point, a lecturer told me to practise using an orange, to develop the basic skill of pushing a needle through the skin.

This is why embalmers need to study the anatomy of the human body, together with learning the practical aspects of embalming. It is crucial that the embalmer knows where the fluid is going to travel in the vascular system. Careful supervision throughout is essential, as if a blockage of any description is encountered, then it will lead to swelling. I know by the changes in colour of the skin that the fluid is slowly seeping into the tissue around the body, as I proceed through the process of embalming. The whole process generally takes around three hours from start to finish, but can take much longer when other challenges arise.

An aspirator is used to remove gases and excessive fluids from the digestive system , which is potentially very problematic if not dealt with correctly, as it can lead to a build-up of gas in the abdomen. Padded underpants or a pad will be used to absorb possible leaks from the bladder.

When a post-mortem has taken place, there are normally sutures in a 'Y' shape stretching from the upper chest to the lower abdomen. This is where the pathologist carried out his or her investigations in order to ascertain the cause of death. It is essential that these sutures are sealed and covered to prevent little leaks that can cause unsightly staining of the clothes of the deceased.

Embalming after a post-mortem has been carried out can be quite tricky. This depends on the level of investigation that had to be undertaken by the pathologist. Sometimes the cause of death can be established at an early stage of the post-mortem. In cases where intensive investigation has been done, there can be a lot of damage to the vascular system, meaning I have to locate different injection sites around the body in order to ensure that the embalming fluid reaches each part of the body.

Post-mortems don't always involve the head. Pathologists are mindful of the need to alleviate any added distress for the bereaved by carefully choosing the less visible areas of the skull when investigating the cause of death. However, sometimes the very cause of death means having an impact on the forehead and facial areas is unavoidable.

It's worth saying here that people are often very upset when an autopsy is needed because of an unexplained sudden death. They often say to me how much they hate the idea of their loved one being cut into like that. I completely understand, of course, why this can feel traumatic, but what I always say to people in this situation is that getting answers about the cause of death can be helpful in the long run, rather than having to live with never knowing. A doctor can say that someone died of a heart attack, but that can be caused by so many things. The line below this on the report is the important one – what brought this on? There have been times when a post-mortem has revealed a hereditary condition that it's as well for the children of the person to be aware of in case they are also affected.

I have been present at and assisted at autopsies. In the 1990s, I often gave talks about my work to various organisations, including the Pathologists Technicians of Ireland. This brought me into contact with the late Professor John Harbison, who was the first state pathologist for Ireland. He was a very impressive man whom I held in high esteem, as he greatly improved pathology services, which were previously terrible in Ireland.

Professor Harbison had almost no resources to work with then, not even an assistant to help him, and he was overloaded with work as he covered the entire country. We had a great conversation one day after I had delivered a talk and he asked if I would be able to assist him when he had an autopsy to perform outside of Dublin. This was when I was in the process of setting up my funeral home, and so I explained that I was very busy with that but promised to help whenever I could. I ended up assisting him a number of times and I learned a lot from him. He was meticulous, always respectful of the dead and incredibly dedicated to his work. He was a fascinating man and was known throughout the country for his work

THE WORK A pathologist needs to do, of course, poses a challenge for an embalmer, but similarly, if a person suffered a long or severe illness prior to death, physical or mental, then this can also hugely impact their appearance. Careful work on my part can mitigate against some of these changes in appearance.

One common problem is discolouration of the face and ears. This can be down to something as simple as the position of the person after they died. Unfortunately, if a person happens to fall forward at the moment of passing, and remains face down for a long duration, this can lead to dark blue discolouration. The same damage is also caused by heart trauma prior to death. This discolouration can be corrected in most cases with careful attention and gentle massage as the fluids circulate around the body. However, it depends on the time that has passed since death. The longer the person is left untreated, the less likely it will be that discolouration can be cleared.

In the case of long delays in the person being released to my care, it is more difficult to get rid of this discolouration and, sadly, in some cases, it is simply not possible to restore the natural pigmentation of the skin. When this is the case, I revert to specialist cosmetics, used by beauticians and created to hide blemishes. These are very sophisticated these days, with plenty of skin tones available. Years ago, I used cosmetics formulated by mortuary suppliers but, over time, I found cosmetics for the living to be far superior to those designed for the deceased.

Open wounds to the person's face or head are a complicated issue. They have to be treated very carefully if there is to be any hope of restoring the person to how they looked in life, and it's important to avoid seepage. They will need to be carefully sutured, or sometimes it is possible to use special glue to close the wound, which can subsequently be covered by a combination of mortuary wax and cosmetics.

If the person has had surgery above the hairline, it can be very difficult to conceal the area, and particularly challenging if the surgery involved the removal of some hair. This is also the case if a post-mortem has required surgery to the head, or if the person had no hair to begin with, as this is really difficult to conceal.

In some cases, the person may have already opted to wear a wig prior to death. Then I can simply replace the wig on the person's head and fashion it as they chose to wear it. Where most of a person's hair still remains on the head, it can be possible to use existing hair cleverly to conceal the wound. I have even had to use hair from the back of the head in order to cover wounds nearer the front hairline. This is a process that takes time and cannot be rushed, but the end result diverts attention from a wound that is difficult to look at and that would imprint a frightening image on the memories of that person's loved ones.

However, facial damage is, as you would expect, much more difficult to conceal than areas covered by hair. We communicate with each other face to face, for the most part. Even if our preferred way of communicating is not to engage through eye contact, it is highly likely that we will notice changes in a person's facial appearance. For many, this is an added trauma contributing mental pain in the course of illness. While staying alive may have been more important than any changes in facial appearance, ultimately, these changes are devastating for the sufferers. Covering of wounds with dressings affords some privacy during that terrible time, but when that person has passed, I feel I have a duty to try to restore their features to what they were, and as the deceased would like others to remember them.

This can be really challenging when some parts of the face have either been removed through surgery or deteriorated badly due to disease. In the case of a terrible accident, parts may have become detached or horrific wounds inflicted In these cases, I use special wax, combined with what is left of the face, to reconstruct the area and bring back the person's natural appearance as best I can. I then use cosmetics to blend the wax with the natural skin tone and texture. In most cases, I can restore the person's appearance; however, there have been times when the damage to the face has been past the point of rescue.

The mouth can take on a different shape depending on how the person died. Intubation, especially over a long period, can distort the shape of the mouth. Structural damage resulting from a collision or blow of some kind to the head will entail a lot of reconstruction to bring back the correct jawline. Without structural support, this part of the face will appear wider and flatter, completely changing the appearance of the person. In some cases, forms can be used to reconstruct areas such as the mouth and eyes.

False teeth have caused me problems over the years too! On many occasions in my early days as an embalmer, I battled with false teeth, trying to fix them in the mouth of the deceased. I have long since learned that a set of false teeth that has not been worn for some time prior to the person's passing is highly unlikely to fit in the mouth properly. I now always ask if they have been recently worn when presented with them, as forms do a much better job than a set of teeth that no longer fits! I have also been presented with clothes that no longer fit the person. Illness can change every facet of our appearance, and our body shape is no exception.

In the case of traumatic sudden deaths, injury can be horrific. Once seen, it is very difficult to erase from memory.

That upsetting image can supersede all other memories of the person. This is really distressing for those who experience it, and unfortunately it is sometimes unavoidable.

I have had to reconstruct large portions of the face in the event of some of these sudden and traumatic deaths. This has even, at times, involved rebuilding structures of the skull. This requires the insertion of special supports where possible, in order to reshape the head. This is an area of work not generally pursued by most embalmers – only a few have specialist training and skill in that field. It is an art in itself, requiring well developed fine motor skills. I have always been drawn towards this kind of specialist work. I have studied it with great interest and have attended many educational sessions dealing specifically with reconstruction of the face and head.

There have been times when, sadly, the challenge of restoring a deceased person's appearance has been so great that I have asked myself if it would be better to just offer the bereaved a closed coffin. I could advise them not to see the person after their passing and just to hold their pre-death memories as they are. It would be far easier for me to do that. However, I believe that, for many, part of the acceptance of a death and embarking on the journey of grief involves knowing first-hand that the person really is forever still. Experiencing that through sight or touch, though harrowing, is very important for many. It is not for me to decide what is best for each individual, but it is my calling to give my best effort to making it possible. It is up to the individual to decide whether or not they want to see or touch the person they loved.

OF COURSE, when preparing the dead for the wake, there are many issues that can arise and must be considered, beyond their outward physical appearance. Many of these are very natural processes but would be very distressing to the bereaved. For example, one potential problem is tissue gas. Tissue gas in a deceased person is a dreaded condition that I have had to deal with on many occasions. It happens when a naturally occurring bacteria in the body becomes very active in the body tissue and spreads rapidly, causing the whole body to swell with gas. The first signs are in the stomach, with discolouration and swelling. This is often accompanied by a terrible odour. All parts of the body begin to be affected, and the condition can get an irreversible grip if not treated. It can lead to seepage of fluids from the body and is very upsetting. Meticulous embalming is required, and great care needs to be taken so the embalmer, or anyone else in contact with the deceased, is not put at risk of infection. Even when the problem has been addressed it can return, so it is vital to keep a close check on the remains to avoid recurrence in any area of the body.

If a person has died as a result of any illness of the liver, they will have a yellow skin tone. I can counteract this through the use a combination of different specialist fluids, but it is essential to get working on this problem as soon as possible after death, as staining can occur that is impossible to reverse.

Oedema is another condition that can be caused by illness, including cancer, heart or kidney failure, the side effects of medications or lack of movement prior to death. In life, fluids are constantly being released into the body's tissues, feeding cells with oxygen and nutrients. At the same time, fluids are absorbed back from the tissues into the circulatory system. This process is called osmosis. When this system ceases to function properly, it can lead to a build-up of fluid in the tissue. Oedema is swelling caused by these extra fluids.

Oedema is a huge challenge for the embalmer and requires great care and caution. A careful assessment needs to be made before deciding on the content and concentration of embalming fluid to be used. It is sometimes possible to reverse the effects of oedema, but there will be times when, despite all efforts, the fluid remains stubbornly in the external tissue of the body.

Something that is upsetting for anyone seeing the deceased to witness but is hard to completely guard against is purging, when fluid comes from the mouth or nose. Even a well-embalmed body can still purge slightly. It is caused by gases that can build up in the abdomen, forcing some of the contents of the stomach to be sent towards the mouth.

Some cotton wool placed in the mouth and upper nostrils usually stops any fluid from escaping.

When I first started to work with the deceased, one of the first realisations for me was that in the few hours after a person dies, changes happen to the body. Algor mortis is a very important process that takes place immediately after death. It is the drop in temperature of the deceased to the ambient temperature of where they passed. If this drop in temperature is hindered in any way, algor mortis will be slowed down. Something as simple as wanting to keep the deceased warm with a quilt can result in the decomposition process commencing far sooner than if the deceased is allowed to cool naturally. This is why it is important to cover the deceased with a light covering such as a sheet, if waiting for a loved one to arrive who wishes to see the deceased before removal from the place of death. The quicker the body is allowed to naturally cool, the better the overall outcome for the presentation of the deceased.

Another thing that also happens in the hours after death is that the body begins to become stiff. This is called rigor mortis: the stiffness of death. If you don't understand it, then the job of dressing and laying out a person on a bed or in a coffin would be very difficult, as the body becomes fixed in whatever position the person was in shortly after death. In the past, nurses, who would often be present when the person died, were trained to wrap bandages around the head to ensure that the mouth closed properly and that the head was in a good position before rigor mortis set in. They also straightened the body on the bed and positioned the hands. Their work was in tandem with the work of the undertaker who followed, and was a huge help, ensuring that the person had a dignified appearance.

But what happens if a person dies suddenly, while sitting, for instance, or in a field, and isn't discovered until several hours later? While rigor mortis can ease naturally with the passing of few days, how can its effects be alleviated in time for a funeral ritual?

It is possible to restore muscular flexibility in the deceased through gentle massage and by slowly flexing the muscles, until they reach a point where the rigor mortis has been removed. Once removed, it won't return. Doing this is essential in order to fix the person into a horizontal position and subsequently dress them. Even when the person has passed away in a horizontal position, flexing and extension of the muscles in the limbs can be necessary, otherwise the deceased can look very rigid and may not have a peaceful presence as a result.

Traditions and religious beliefs around how the person's hands and arms are positioned in the coffin vary. Some require the arms to be placed alongside the body, while others prefer hands to be joined. When the hands are going to be visible to mourners, it is important that they look well. Many people visiting a funeral like to touch the person's hands for that last time, in a final act of farewell. In most cases, the colour of the hands will clear up well during the process of embalming, but sometimes hands can be difficult to get right. This all depends on conditions prior to death.

Sometimes the task is as easy as just washing the hands carefully and massaging as fluid is injected. However, there are times when there is discolouration of the skin of the hands, perhaps caused by circulation issues prior to death or the position of a cannula from hospital treatments. If the circulatory routes through the veins have collapsed, then it can be difficult to get hygienic fluid through to all areas of the hands. Sometimes, in the case of injuries resulting from falls, there can be staining through bruises that haven't healed. When the colour of the hands doesn't clear, it is necessary to resort to cosmetics to conceal the discolouration.

Of course, it is important to pay attention to the nails, making sure that they are clean. If the person often wore nail colours in life then I will paint the nails. Family members have often requested to do the nails of their loved one themselves, which I am always open to as I feel it is helpful for the bereaved to engage in something that they did for that person in life. It is an important task that brings some solace.

I often have to remove rings from the fingers of the deceased person. If they were someone who never took off their rings this can be a difficult task, but with perseverance and some cream, I usually succeed in removing the treasured jewellery to return to the person's relatives.

It has not been unusual, over the years, to have the person's hairdresser or barber fix their hair, as they always did it for them in life. Sometimes, family members request to do this too. The only problem they all encounter is that they are unlikely to have ever styled that person's hair while they were lying down! Unless, of course, that person had been confined to bed for a long time. A good hairdresser or barber usually gets over the problem with ease.

It is very important to get a person's hair right, as a bad hair do can change someone's appearance completely. Some of us like to change our hairstyles over the years, so photos of the most preferred hairstyle are a huge help. I have had the misfortune of working with an older photo of a person with a totally different hairstyle. When the bereaved saw the hair, they didn't hesitate to tell me how wrong it looked! The photos given to the embalmer really matter, so it's important to make sure that they are up to date.

Once a person is laid out in the coffin, with hair and make-up all done, they are ready to be placed in the funeral home or taken home to their residence, the residence of a family member or neighbour for the wake, allowing the bereaved to spend time in their presence. The wake is typically held over one or two nights and days. Sometimes it can be longer if mourners have to travel to say goodbye. I have witnessed delays of over a week on many occasions and, depending on weather conditions, it can be difficult to continue to maintain the visual appearance of the deceased.

Once the person is in position for the wake, attention needs to be given to some details in the room. In the summer months in particular, flies are not unusual, especially if the weather is a little warmer than normal. However, they are a huge threat to the body of a deceased person. To put it crudely, it's nature's way of getting started on decomposition. The natural lifecycle of a fly involves laying eggs that subsequently grow into larvae, and the rest I will leave to your imagination when it comes to the deceased person. If present, they tend to appear around the orifices of the head. Seeing larvae on the deceased is, of course, very distressing. What is particularly frightening to the living is that they appear to come from within the person, when in actual fact, they are the result of eggs being deposited near to the openings of the orifices by flies in the room; they are usually superficial rather than deep inside the person. So it is best to avoid any possibility of flies getting anywhere near the deceased in the first place. Cotton wool placed in the upper nose and in the mouth prevents flies from getting into the body, but the best way to protect the deceased is to drape a piece of net fabric over the entire coffin, removing it from time to time when no flies are in the room.

Recovering the Deceased

IN MY COMMUNITY, we live and work on the Atlantic coastline, with rivers in most of our main towns. These waters can be a great source of joy for us, but, sadly, they can also be a cause of great pain for many.

Over the years, I have seen many people lost to these waters, either through accident or a decision to escape terrible mental torture. Either way, it is better if the remains can be located and taken from the water as soon as possible. When someone is reported missing and it's suspected they may be in the water, communities turn out in full force to assist in searches and give their time and energy with such goodness. In rare cases, adverse weather conditions lead to the deceased being carried far away to another place, sometimes never to be recovered.

The Gardaí (the Irish police) must be called when someone dies suddenly. I get the call from the Gardaí to attend the scene when their investigations are complete.

I have received this dreaded call on many occasions, and gone to meet with dedicated volunteers of sub-aqua clubs and rescue services when the remains of a deceased person have finally been located. It marks the end of a search, closure for the bereaved and relief that their loved one has been found and that they can be afforded a funeral ritual. However, there remains the question of what state the body of their loved one will have been left in.

Sometimes when found in water, remains can be unharmed. Other times, unfortunately, the currents have travelled in conflicting directions, leading to a lot of damage to the remains. The main concerns for an embalmer when working with a person who has been taken from a river or the sea is that organisms may have entered the body after death, and this can cause complications. Swelling may have occurred and, worse still, bruising and even mutilation of the body. The whole embalming process can be quite complex, especially if salt water has been absorbed into the body.

At the very least, the person's appearance improves when the body is washed and dressed. After that, each individual person is different, depending on the circumstances. Sometimes it is possible to reverse damage done, and at other times, it can be virtually impossible. But I always try.

I have experienced many occasions when it has taken the authorities many months to establish the identity of the deceased, when their remains have been washed ashore a long way from where that person first entered the water. It is not unusual for them to have been drawn out to sea with the current and returned to shore by the ocean at her chosen destination. In rivers, underwater ledges can provide refuge for remains until their presence is revealed by a drought or a flood brings them swiftly downstream.

I have been called to remove deceased persons who have been dead for many days. In some cases, the person was found outdoors, where they had passed suddenly. It is always a very sad and grim sight to attend, and particularly painful for those closest to the deceased. Some of them may have been actively searching for the deceased, whereas for others, the deceased may have been a very private person who often went away for long periods. They may have had a second residence or friends they often visited, which meant they had been dead for some time before being missed.

Depending on weather conditions, and where the person is found, we can then be faced with all kinds of complications. Sometimes just reaching the deceased with a stretcher can be really challenging – for example, during the winter months when fields can be very wet and sometimes flooded. Trolleys are not built for such terrain, so that is not an option. If the ground is muddy, then you have problems like literally getting stuck in the muck, and also the danger of slipping as you transfer the person to a stretcher to bring them to the ambulance or hearse. This transfer could entail crossing several fields on foot to get back to the road. In the winter months, time is against us, as the hours of daylight are much shorter. In these circumstances, I have always found that farmers from the area will step up to the mark, sharing their knowledge of the land, enabling us to exit by the most accessible route, helping to preserve the dignity of the deceased person. The Gardaí are also a great help in these situations.

As I live and work on the coast, it's probably to be expected that I have looked after deceased on ships. A ship can be quite a dangerous place if you happen to be in the wrong place at the wrong time in the midst of a serious storm at sea. Some deceased people I have recovered from ships had died from injuries sustained in this manner, while others passed from natural causes, or experienced medical problems, but it wasn't possible to get them to a hospital on land in time.

Sudden deaths on board a ship come with unique complications. For one, there can be delays in repatriation of the person who has died, especially if the ship is many days away from the shore. The deceased may also be far from their homeland, due to the global nature of the shipping industry. Even simply removing sailors who have died at sea can be a very difficult task, not least when you consider the small passages in ships' crew quarters.

I have found it to be very sad to be involved in the repatriation of sailors who may not have seen their families for several months. Their belongings tell you that they have loved ones at home, often in a far-off place. It really sinks in when you label their few possessions to accompany the hermitically sealed coffin and bring them to the airport for their final journey home. In some cases, the person is cremated, with the permission of their next of kin, but this means that loved ones never get to see that person again.

One young man will always stand out in my mind. He was cremated before being sent home to his country on the other side of the world. All I could think of was his heartbroken parents and siblings, who would have parted with a healthy young man, setting out to explore the world through travelling its oceans, full of enthusiasm and hope, possibly generously sending home gifts over the months. I felt the need to look after this person for his family and mind him for them. I remember cutting some of his hair, which was very short, and placing it in an envelope along with a photo taken of him in the coffin prior to cremation. I wanted them to have the option of seeing him in a peaceful state in the hope that it would be of some consolation to them. The envelope was placed carefully in his duffel bag that was being returned with his cremated remains. I will never know if this was a consolation to his loved ones but my intention was to try to help them have some closure. These sudden deaths have to be really difficult for the bereaved, not least when you consider the long waiting period before someone can be brought home.

Sudden deaths often occur from accidental causes or from natural causes. However, I have seen many that were caused by the person themselves. I have often had to recover someone's remains after they decided to exit this life in a self-determined way, and have witnessed many different approaches to this. It's a very difficult task to face.

I get a sick feeling in my stomach when I get a call from the Gardaí (who have to attend the scene) and they tell me that the deceased had elected to use a rope. More often than not, I have the arduous task of taking down the poor soul, who had not been able to continue in this life. This is a truly terrible task, but it has to be done, and with as much respect as possible, despite the fact that the location may be difficult to get to. I have had to do this many times in hay sheds and outbuildings.

It breaks my heart when I arrive to a scene where a family member or someone close to the person has already managed to take them down in a desperate attempt to save them from death. The action taken by the deceased usually appears to have been well planned, but carried out in a split second and totally irreversible, bringing with it terrible heartbreak. It is horrible to hear the trembling sobs of grief of those who loved that person as they stand helplessly by.

In many cases, it can be next to impossible to reach the area where a rope has been connected, but there is often pressure to try to get the person lowered down before others close to the deceased arrive, to spare them from having that terrible memory imprinted forever on their minds.

The sense of pain can be felt by all present. There are no words that can ease the heartache felt in those moments. Offering physical presence, support and empathy is the best we can do, while uttering private prayers seeking comfort for these distraught people to help them cope, one day at a time, without a person who was very dear to them. I have witnessed all kinds of emotional responses and disbelief at what has happened.

It is an equally harrowing experience for all concerned when a person has used a very violent method, resulting in a lot of blood loss, in the process of ending it all. The area may have to be cordoned off for forensic reasons, to ensure that there has been no foul play. Bereaved people wait helplessly as Gardaí protect the scene, awaiting the arrival of the pathologist. This may take several hours, depending on location, and, subsequently, there may be delays in establishing the cause of death. Gardaí specialising in forensics have to record the scene in detail. This is very distressing for the bereaved, who watch from a distance, desperately wanting to hold and mind their loved one.

Fortunately, nowadays, at least the area can be covered with a forensic work tent, affording privacy and protection from the elements and more dignity for the deceased. Decades ago, this work was often carried out in the open air, and the deceased was covered with a blanket until the appropriate personnel arrived.

Death by suicide preys on the mind and spirit. Oddly, we can all empathise to a certain degree, when we remind ourselves of our lowest days, if we have ever suffered from depression. I shudder to think of the number of people that any of us could potentially affect, if, having this terrible illness, we were to take that irreversible action.

I once saved a person from drowning. I am not a strong swimmer, and the cold water of the river was a shock to the system. Several weeks later, when we met again, to my surprise, the person chastised me for preventing them from taking their own life. I hadn't thought of it that way. As far as they were concerned, I had caused their pain to continue. I tried my best to point out reasons for living, but my words were of little consolation. We parted company on friendly terms and I felt that a good deed had been achieved. Alas, that person only managed to endure life for a few more weeks after that. I will always remember our conversation, as well as my subsequent sense of helplessness on hearing that my attempts had been futile. However, I would never have forgiven myself if I hadn't tried.

It's true that I have on occasion sensed great peace around someone who had died by suicide, and this could only be a sign to me that they had experienced terrible mental suffering prior to death.

Exiting this life by choice might end pain and suffering for the deceased person, but, as I have experienced through working with the bereaved, there is a huge chasm created as people try to cope with an irreconcilable loss. In many cases, those close to the deceased will have made several attempts to help that person deal with their sense of total hopelessness. But it's true that talking about suicidal thoughts can be extremely difficult for the sufferer and equally challenging for the listener.

Sometimes, thoughts are shared in a flippant way without arousing suspicion or danger. Other times, suicidal thoughts are clearly verbalised prior to death. Most of us are ill equipped to handle these conversations and fumble through, trying to help the sufferer to think positively about living. There is often only one chance at this conversation, so how can we have any hope of getting it right first time, with no chance to premeditate our possible response? I have met many bereaved people who replay conversations, exploring alternative things that they might have done, but how could they have predicted with certainty the way things would play out?

In Ireland, we can be awkward about telling our loved ones how much we love, respect and care for them. It tends to be more of a 'Sure, you know we love you very much!'. We are not good at talking about these emotions. It's a curious way to be, and I can't explain why we are like this, but we need to change. Little by little, we are beginning to learn how to express our feelings of love and respect for people close to us. Our younger generation have been encouraged to be more open in talking about their feelings. Education and social media have helped this. This is really important.

I have come across many deaths by suicide where the death comes completely out of the blue, with no warning signs. This is particularly heart-breaking, as the person has suffered in silence, unable to talk about their melancholy, and managed to conceal their pain. Any case of a sudden death of this kind brings terribly mixed-up emotions for those who are bereaved. Pain, anger, sorrow, but most of all a great sense of the loss of a person who is still deeply loved. Questions torment the abandoned, never to be answered.

Having seen the pain caused by this sort of loss first-hand, many times over, I appeal to anyone suffering that kind of pain to continue to seek help, and to not give up until they find a person they can connect with and trust. It can be really difficult to have these conversations with those closest to us, it's true, but if this is the case, try to find a professional person or counsellor to help you work through difficult thoughts. Not every counsellor will suit you, so keep searching until you find the one that you 'click' with and can talk to with ease.

Friends and family can also help, but you have to let down the barriers and allow them into your world. Suicide is not the only way out, so don't give up if you are feeling very down; you have no idea of how many people really love and care for you, even if they don't always know what to do or say for the best.

I have met lots of people who have recovered from debilitating depression and are thankful that they were diverted from that path, which would have led to self-destruction.

*

WHEN IT COMES TO sudden death, one cannot ignore the horrific accidents that take place on our roads. I have been called in the middle of the night to the scenes of terrible road traffic accidents. We have searched fields around accidents, not knowing if there were others in the crash who may have been thrown from the vehicle. Worse still, I have taken people from cars that overturned and landed in a shallow drain, trapping the vehicle's occupants, who drowned.

It is heart-breaking to have to bring a person back to their home that they left only the day before full of fun and energy. There are no words that can console the bereaved as you arrange the coffin. You can only quietly leave, with the devastated mourners often in a daze, unable to talk to anyone. It is even more difficult when there are multiple deaths involved. I have been called to scenes when more than one family member has died in the same crash. Sometimes a whole community is plunged into mourning, and everyone offers their help, and does whatever it is they can do.

I have given talks to secondary school students to encourage teenagers to appreciate the dangers on the road and the importance of taking great care when they begin to take to the road as young drivers.

I can only try to imagine the deep sense of loss experienced by parents who lose their children in road traffic accidents, at any age. I have also witnessed the helplessness and deep regret of drivers who survived crashes in which a passenger or occupant of another vehicle died. Unanswered questions and what ifs abound. It might even have been the reckless driving of another driver that caused the accident, or unexpected weather conditions, or the involvement of speed, drugs or alcohol. No matter how it is viewed, or whose actions caused it, a vehicle went out of control, on their watch. The consequences can never be fixed, which is, in itself, a life sentence for that driver.

I once had to look after a mother and daughter who were killed in a horrific accident on the last day of a wonderful holiday here with relations. They were not from Ireland, and were due to be flying home to Germany on the day of the tragic accident.

My own daughters were teenagers at that time, and I was weak to the core imagining myself in the same scenario as that poor father and husband. It was truly unbearable to think that only a few hours ago, he had been expecting them home, laughing and full of joy, bearing Irish gifts for everyone, and now he awaited a different homecoming. How could he possibly ever get over such a loss? I had collected the mother and daughter from the hospital with their belongings. I then had the horrific task of getting them ready for a different journey home.

As I worked, I heard a phone beeping. It was beeping every few minutes and I couldn't think where it was coming from. I looked around the mortuary, first thinking that the phone belonged to one of my employees, but then discovered it in the bag with the belongings of the young girl. I later discovered from her family that the beeps were messages coming in from her friends, who eagerly awaited her return from her holiday and were expecting to see her soon to catch up with all of the news.

That really hit a nerve with me. My own daughters were no different to that girl who lay still before me. They were young, full of life and fun, and their phones were constantly beeping. I felt sick at the very thought of anything happening to my girls, and yet none of us can ever be sure it won't. We need to enjoy each other's company while we still have time together.

On another occasion, I remember a young teacher who had driven all the way from Scotland for mid-term break with his family in Ireland and was tragically killed when he tried to overtake a bus that he had been driving behind for a long stretch of road. He was excited about getting home but was a careful driver. At one point, he moved out slightly to see if it was safe to overtake the bus and, due to his unfortunate timing, the car was clipped by an oncoming lorry. He was killed instantly.

Meanwhile, his mother was looking forward to his home-coming. He had called her from the ferry port when he had landed in Ireland, so she had an idea of what time he should be home by. She had cooked the full Irish breakfast for him, and it was in the oven ready as she awaited his arrival. Instead of his cheerful greeting, she was met at the door by two Gardaí, and before they said anything, she knew some-thing terrible had happened. He was the couple's only son and his loss was devastating for them.

It was such a sad time for everyone. His teaching col-leagues from Scotland came for his funeral, and many of his young pupils were brought over by their parents. It was a great tribute to him as a person to be remembered so fondly by his pupils and colleagues. I always think of him any time I drive on that stretch of road, and consider how one instant can change everything.

On another occasion, a young driver died tragically, but not because of her driving. She died in the passenger seat of her own car. A friend had offered to drive and didn't drink alcohol at all on the night. It was a lovely moonlit night, but the road conditions were unexpectedly treach-erous due to a hard frost. The car went completely out of control and hit a wall, and she was killed instantly. She was a well-liked young woman, and thousands turned out to her funeral. The hurt of families in this situation is terrible. The young person had done the right thing but ended up losing her life. Treacherous and unexpected black ice has been the cause of many terrible fatal crashes, especially in late autumn when the winter weather starts to snap in on deceptively beautiful nights.

It again brings home the preciousness of life itself, and the importance of making the most of every day spent with people we love and respect.

When a sudden death of any kind has taken place, it is not just a case of me arriving and having to face a terrible situation. A whole network of professionals forms very quickly.

Members of the Gardaí are truly to be commended for their outstanding work. It is at times like these that you realise that theirs is not merely a job, but a true vocation and calling to help others. I have met so many members of the force who go way beyond the call of duty to assist in any way possible, their ultimate aim being that of respect and maintaining the dignity of the deceased during the removal of a person's remains from the scene, wherever that may be. They are usually also involved in making contact with those closest to the deceased. Delivering the worst possible news to someone is a really difficult task, requiring more than any training can ever prepare you for. It involves empathy, support and kindness.

Doctors also often have the daunting task of attending the scene. It is harrowing for them when they struggle and fail to save the person. They do a terrific job in difficult circumstances, and often have to deal with the trauma that follows for them.

The clergy also play a vital role in answering calls to the scene of an accident. Over the years, I have seen that they have been there for the bereaved on the night of the tragedy, and have gone on to support them in the days, months and sometimes years that follow in the journey of bereavement.

Firefighters, sub-aqua clubs, the RNLI, the Irish coastguard and other first responders also come through with the same valour and dedication – not only in their work, but as members of the community supporting the bereaved in the most appropriate way possible.

Following a car accident, firefighters often have to cut vehicles to free both the living and the dead from wreckage. They also have the arduous task of removing victims from the scenes of fires, which is really dangerous work.

Sub-aqua clubs work from dawn to dusk, looking for souls missing in our rivers and seas. They search the dark, murky waters of our rivers in awful conditions, not knowing where a person is going to be discovered.

The RNLI provides access to otherwise unreachable areas along our coast, often discovering deceased persons washed ashore in remote places that are very hard to access.

Many have paid the ultimate price in dangerous seas as they gave selflessly of themselves to save others. The Irish coastguard work generously in the same way, always wanting to save lives or, failing that, bring closure by locating the remains of loved ones after tragedy has struck.

Ambulance staff act quickly, providing vital support for severely injured persons who have managed to survive a road collision or other accident. They save lives through their quick response and actions. Those moments of sustaining life, helped by the advice of a doctor either present or on the phone, are the difference between life and death for many victims of accidents.

Many of the people who attend these tragic scenes suffer sleepless nights, struggling with nightmares of the dreaded scene they have visited. In many cases, they cannot talk openly to others of their experience. Their dedication to preserving the dignity of the deceased prevents them from discussing it, not to mention the confidential nature of their work. Many of us don't even think about this side of their jobs.

I know all too well the trauma these people suffer in the days and months following these tragedies, as there is an understanding between all who have attended these disturbing scenes that there are simply no words to explain what has been witnessed. Many cope with the trauma through counselling. On many occasions, we have shared our methods of coping with such tragedies, of finding ways to accept that we did our best in unprecedented circumstances that we had no control over. I meet these professionals and volunteers in passing at funerals, and one look communicates our mutual pain.

Things I Have Learned About Grief

I ENCOUNTER GRIEF every day of the week in my work. On some days, it is through the painful cries of loss from a bereaved person; on other days, it is through chatting to someone who, several years after losing a person very dear to them, still feels that pain as badly as the day they first received the dreadful news or witnessed the passing of the person they so loved. I have even seen this deep hurt lead to physical illness. Things like anxiety, loss of appetite or total neglect of symptoms of an illness due to grief can be devastating. We hope that with support, a bereaved person can find some way of coping with their loss, continuing to live, even while bearing that terrible pain. Sometimes that pain can be forgotten temporarily as we immerse ourselves in life. Sometimes it takes a long time to get to this point.

In this chapter and the next, I will talk about my experiences of grief and how we can deal with it, personally and in communities. If you are currently struggling with loss and grief, you may find this section painful, and should feel free to skip to the next section.

I remember a family of seven coming to make arrangements for their late mother who had died quite suddenly following an illness. The tensions were high in the room as we discussed the funeral arrangements. They were, of course, in the early stages of their grief. Some family members blamed their father for not making their mother go to the doctor when she first became ill. He said she wouldn't go, that she thought she wasn't bad enough. Others blamed the doctors. One daughter was grateful that her mother had been spared the torture of treatment for her particular illness, and believed that God was good to her. A son was in total misery because his last words with his late mother, before the ambulance took her to hospital, had been about dumping his dirty dishes in the kitchen sink. She had asked him to wash them and he had replied, as was usual for him, that he would do them later, something that always drove her mad. Not an ideal final conversation for the records.

Another daughter was reminiscing on how good their mother was, how she had always done her best for them. Her way of dealing with her grief was wanting the most expensive send-off possible for her mother. You can imagine the response she got from her siblings as her demands became more and more outrageous.

Making arrangements in such circumstances can be a very slow process. When people are grieving the loss of someone they love and care about, they are very sensitive and full of myriad emotions. In this instance, the family had to be given time to work things out in their own way, with me interceding from time to time to keep everything moving. At one stage, I had to leave the room and let them work it out as siblings.

Even picking their mother's outfit took a lot of deliberation. They meticulously compared photos before finally agreeing on how her hair should be styled. Make-up and jewellery proved to be another bone of contention.

The dispute over whether or not to cremate their mother was resolved by their dad, who said he didn't want to be cremated when he died, and that he wanted to be laid to rest beside his soulmate in a grave that friends and relatives could visit.

Not all families have such differences, but it's not unusual for there to be disagreements at this time. Grief takes its toll in many ways. This is why it can be a very difficult process working through the stages of a funeral with the bereaved. Everyone is grieving differently and emotions are high. Family members and friends of the deceased who, under normal circumstances, are really close can bitterly dispute what afterwards seems irrelevant.

I try to help them to navigate this difficult time, encouraging them to give each other space and to get to a point where they can agree and make decisions. I try not to get involved in the differences of opinion, and instead focus on the task at hand, encouraging all parties to make allowances for the grief they are all going through in different ways.

Many suffer their grief in silence and do their best to keep up a brave front for others around them. Others are inconsolable and never manage to live life to its fullest again in the aftermath of the loss of someone who was a huge part of their very being and existence. There are those whose religious beliefs help them to fully accept the passing of someone important in their lives.

I remember one man telling me that he never got over the death of his wife, who had died suddenly a long time ago. He was always well-groomed and donned a hat as he rode his Honda 50, a motorbike dating back to the seventies that was used as a common mode of transport in rural areas. He told me that when his wife died, he didn't even know where his socks were kept. So when all had settled down after the funeral, he had to search for his socks, finding them in the hot press in the place neatly allocated for them. His wife had attended to those details, and he in turn had looked after other chores. They had a rhythm of living that worked for both of them. He was terribly lonely after she died, and his life was completely out of balance. Fortunately, his neighbours were a huge support, and he was lucky to have most of his family in the region. They called on him often.

I worry most about those who remain calm and composed throughout the funeral ritual. They keep everyone on task and look after most of the negotiations, some of which are extremely difficult and painful. They somehow manage to hide it away. I don't think that they have any control over this reaction to their trauma. At some unknown future date, something rips open that hiding place, forcing everything out into the open. This can often mean that they begin their grief journey at a time when others around them have reached some stage of acceptance of the loss, meaning they feel they are grieving alone, and sometimes even feel bitter that others do not appear to be missing the person as much as they are at that time.

Everyone experiences grief at some stage in life. We all exit this life through death. There are always going to be people left on this earth suffering in grief. I might add that grief also accompanies other profound losses in our lives – for example, the loss of the ability to use a part of our body due to illness or an accident, or the loss of a friend or family member through emigration. There are lots of things that cause us to feel grief, but death is final, and there is no escaping the fact that it can bring with it profound and enduring sadness.

We can all try to imagine our reaction to a death, but until it actually happens, we have no idea of how we will behave. Our behaviour can be affected by others around us, and even the cause of death itself. Unpredictable responses from others who are close to us can throw us out of kilter. When we are in a spin, we have no understanding of those unexpected responses. We are not thinking rationally. We can become very angry during this time when we cannot see the wood for the trees. Sudden, shocking losses can affect us differently from a death that we have had time to at least attempt to prepare ourselves for, when the person we lose has been ill for a long time or was very old at the time of their passing. But however we experience it, a loss is a loss and will have a profound impact.

I was young and hadn't yet experienced death on a personal level when I went to Chicago to gain more knowledge and skills in my vocation. Little did I know that I would be going through grief myself within a few short years.

When my uncle Mike passed away in 1989, I was devastated. We had several common interests. He was my mentor and I thoroughly enjoyed his company. He thrived on doing good in his community and was the driving force behind many different initiatives in the area. He always encouraged me to do the same. Lots of us have ideas, but when we share them with the right person, they come to full fruition. It was like that for me with my uncle. I still miss him.

He was younger than I am now when he passed away, following a few months in hospital. Throughout his illness, there were many times when I had great hope for his recovery. I suppose I envisaged everyone helping him through a recovery process. I did not want to think that he may be gone from us forever, and that I would never again be able to have those interesting chats with him.

He was a great loss to his community, but most of all to his family.

As I have said, I was ignorant to the importance of studying sociology and psychology in relation to funerals when I began my course in Chicago. It's strange now to think that I even considered dropping these subjects altogether because I saw no value in them at that time. And while, unfortunately, there is no substitute for going on that journey ourselves if we are to truly understand the depth of the psychological wound inflicted on us by death, studying those subjects turned out to be core to understanding my role in the grief journey as a funeral director and embalmer, and I am glad that I didn't abandon them.

The more I studied the psychology of grief, the more I realised how intertwined grief is with the way the deceased is prepared for their loved ones for the funeral ritual. It made so much sense to me. I was so wrapped up in getting the embalming and presentation right, that, prior to this, I hadn't considered how important it was in the big picture.

As I have continued in my career, I have read many articles to help me try to understand grief. I want to help people as I watch them attempt to cope with such change in their lives. Most people have heard of the five stages of grief, which were identified by psychiatrist Elizabeth Kübler-Ross in her very influential book *On Death and Dying* in 1969:

Denial
Anger
Bargaining
Depression
Acceptance

Kübler-Ross identified grief in lots of different instances, not solely relating to death but also the different losses that we experience throughout our lives. Her work opened up discussion and debate on the topic. In her later work, she acknowledged that people do not necessarily experience grief in any particular order, as she had first thought. Some may not experience all of these stages, either.

This appears to me to be true – the ways in which we grieve are personal to us and our circumstances – but from what I have seen in my work as a funeral director, I can identify with her theories.

So many people experience denial, especially when the death is sudden and the bereaved are not in the same place as the person who has died. They cling on to the false hope that someone has got it wrong. That their loved one is going to come through the door any minute, or text or phone, or listen to that phone message left for them.

I have met people who are very angry at the loss of their loved one. There can be numerous reasons for this.

The worst I have ever come across is the murder of a person, but there are other reasons for feelings of anger after death comes to the door.

People who have always tried to be good citizens often cannot understand why this has happened to them. Some question God and their religious belief systems, wondering how a loving God could inflict such pain.

All kinds of feelings of guilt can come into play. People dwell on the missed chances – what could have been if they had not gone somewhere, not done something, or just done something differently. This brings sheer torture to the bereaved, and for some it can never be fully resolved. They play scenarios over and over in their minds, believing that if they had done something differently, their loved one might still be alive. Alas, no matter how many times the scenarios are replayed, there is no return from death. These thoughts achieve nothing but to serve huge portions of pain to the sufferer.

We cannot replay a day or a night. We can't travel back in time. We have to allow others to help us to put it behind ourselves and change our focus.

Many say that a year is a modest amount of time for a person to really grieve. A year gives us time to go through every part of the year, involving traditions, anniversaries, family gatherings, birthdays, etc., without that loved one being there. In bygone days, it was normal for bereaved people in the West of Ireland to wear black for a year following the death of an immediate family member – or, at the very least, for a few months. Black attire reminded everyone in the community to be mindful of the grief that the person was going through. Support was given freely within the community and allowances were made. People were discouraged from making important decisions during that period.

In a strange way, the feeling of grief can be a comfort sometimes. I suppose when you think about it, grief is the last emotion you associate with the deceased. That feeling of grief, can, strangely enough, bring a sense of closeness again with the person who is gone.

It is all too easy to feel guilty about beginning to live again after the loss of someone special. The act of just smiling or even feeling happy for a moment can bring dreadful feelings of betrayal and remorse. This is normal, but how many of us would want anyone to continue suffering indefinitely after we are gone from their lives? We might not want to be forgotten, but would we really want someone to be tortured by our departure for the rest of their days?

I often meet people who are deeply depressed as a result of grief. I have spent hours talking to people who suffer because of the loss of a very special person in their lives. Talking to others helps. As a funeral director, I have opportunities to visit the bereaved following the funeral, and these visits afford me the chance to stop and spend some time with these people. People often pop into the funeral home for a chat with someone who has travelled the funeral journey with them. Some of those who are suffering with depression will tell me how they cope through talking to friends or seeing counsellors, which is good to hear. It doesn't take much for any of us in our communities to remember a person who is grieving and to make a special effort to call for a chat, to invite them for a walk or to do something with them that helps them to gradually begin to live in the aftermath of the loss of someone they loved dearly. We need to help each other. I have seen so often how important this is. Sometimes someone who is not even necessarily close to the bereaved will step in and include them in activities where they meet different people, giving them space to be themselves without carrying a huge sense of guilt, in places where there are no prior memories, enabling the creation of new ones. We will all suffer grief at some point. 'What goes around, comes around,' as the saying goes, and the support we offer will surely be returned within a caring community.

Acceptance of death is very difficult. Belief systems can play a vital role in getting to this stage. Different faiths offer support to the bereaved and help them come to terms with the void in their lives. It can take a really long time to finally come to accept the death of someone so close to us. And even then, grief can stay within us, a bit like an imaginary Pandora's box. We can keep it closed most of the time, but, at some point, there will be things that will force it open. It may be a piece of music, a song. It may be special items that have been kept, or it might be going to a particular place. Whatever it is, the memories will come flooding back once that little box is opened. It affords the opportunity for a good cry. When the pain subsides, tears are wiped away, and Pandora's box is closed once more and stored safely near the heart.

I don't know if time can ever heal the broken-hearted, but time can help us to accept the changes inflicted by loss. Somehow, time allows us to be able to set grief aside and continue living. Our own Pandora's box means we will never forget, and forgetting someone is something we probably never want to do anyway. We know we have the emotions of the loss stashed away, but we reach a point where we can live with that, while knowing that even if we don't feel those same emotions and think of the person we have lost all the time, we would never forget someone so dear and important to us. This can help us to continue living without feeling guilty.

Making Arrangements

Memory is a funny thing. Our senses have the ability to bring us right back even to a distant memory. Smells that accompanied pleasant moments from the past can bring those memories and emotions right back to us. Images also bring us back to occasions from the past, and there is nothing like a song, music or poetry to evoke memories. Our minds can store the emotional connections with these different things in ways that can be unpredictable and sometimes hard to explain.

Death engraves memories on our brains that never go away. For example, we may remember with great clarity where we were and what we were doing when we heard of someone's death. Particular scents, emotions, images or something somebody said to us during a funeral can stay with us forever.

Strangely, for many people, their final vision of a person they loved dearly is the one that can precede all other images of that person for them. That is not to say that they forget other images of the person that they had – it's simply that their brains often inadvertently retain that image in the number-one slot in their memory.

This is why my work is so important to individuals who are grieving. It means a lot to the bereaved to see someone they have lost forever looking comfortable and at their best for the very last time. Some disagree, saying they're gone and that's it, but I believe that what you see that last time is extremely important. I believe that it helps the recently bereaved to begin to process everything that has been thrown at them. We are so sensitive and dealing with so much at this time that this final encounter must be made as comfortable and reassuring as possible. That is why the work of the funeral director and the embalmer is so important.

How many of us have spent many hours getting ready for a special occasion, like a wedding or another important celebration? We carefully prepare a suitable outfit and accessories, and we then attend to grooming, getting our hair cut or styled. On the day of the event, we take even more time attending to the details, getting ready to meet everyone, thinking of the possibility of photographs with friends and acquaintances whose company we enjoy and with whom we want to create good memories, that we can revisit in the future, reconnecting us with moments of great joy.

Making Arrangements

We most certainly would not be happy to be dragged from the garden, in our gardening attire, covered in soil, to be brought straight into a smart room full of people dressed in their best. Yet, that could be the scenario when someone dies and has no control over how they will look as they lie among others who are dressed in their best as a mark of respect for their very funeral.

It is up to the funeral director, who is charged with the responsibility of caring for the deceased, to look after their needs. The funeral director, the embalmer and all other staff involved are there to ensure that this person is afforded the same respect and attention that the eager salesperson in a fashion shop gives us when we prepare for a special occasion.

In my work, I see it as my duty to afford the dead respect and empathy. I see it as an insult to the bereaved and to the deceased not to make my best efforts to try to help the deceased get ready for the last special occasion in their lives. It is important to remember that no good outfit of clothes, make-up or hairdo will substitute for the work carried out by the embalmer. The embalmer plays the most important role in preparing the deceased for this process. A good embalmer is a vital member of staff for a funeral director.

*

SOME PEOPLE PREFER to plan their own funerals. On many occasions, I have worked with someone who has accepted their terminal diagnosis and has decided to make their own funeral arrangements. It is a very surreal task for that person and for me.

I feel it is very important to be practical and thorough. Some things can be carefully planned in every detail, such as the clothes they want to be laid out in, the type of coffin, whether they want to be cremated or if they are to be buried, and where this is to take place. Other things can be far more difficult to plan as they may become impossible to fulfil at the time of death. For example, someone may request a particular singer for the final ritual, and it may turn out that they are not available on the day of the funeral. I have seen similar problems arise where certain celebrants were requested by the person but were engaged elsewhere. Sometimes, people have been selected by the person to say prayers or readings, but these people found themselves emotionally unable to get up in front of everyone on the day of the funeral. If specified tasks or requests are unable to be fulfilled, it can put much pressure on the bereaved, who may feel they are letting down their loved one by not honouring their wishes, even though it is out of their control.

When someone goes over their arrangements with me, I usually ensure this is witnessed or shared, with permission, with someone close who will be around as the moment of death approaches. Alternatively, a record of the details signed by the person can help alleviate unexpected disputes over the wishes of the dying person at a later time. All too often, I have seen well-intentioned people turn up, who haven't been present throughout, and cause havoc by introducing their opinion on how things should be carried out for the funeral. This can be very disturbing for those present who were very much aware of the wishes of the deceased.

OVER MY TIME as a funeral director and embalmer, I have seen many changes to the way funerals are organised in Ireland. For example, the funeral may not take place so quickly after the person has passed now, as embalming means that period can be prolonged if necessary – for example, if some of the family have to travel. It remained common in the West of Ireland to take the deceased to church on the night before the funeral to be left overnight there up until the pandemic, though this has been less popular in recent years. I think this changed as people were so often denied the opportunity to say goodbye during the lockdowns that many found that when they could, they wanted to spend as much time as possible with the deceased. Many people nowadays opt to use the funeral home for the repose for the bereaved, where everyone can come and pay their respects, and then bring the deceased home for the rest of the time, sometimes keeping the house private for relatives and close friends.

The community doesn't come to a standstill as it once did when someone passed. Sadly, as our workplaces became more advanced, so too did the rules about people leaving work to go to funerals. That's not to say that there isn't still huge community support of the bereaved these days, though. Far from it. Neighbours will come to give their help when the wake is being held at the house, making sandwiches and cakes, and organising parking and dealing with traffic near the house where needed. Loyalty to the bereaved is still strong in this regard, and people still turn out in large numbers to pay their respects, form a guard of honour or walk with the hearse on the deceased's final journey. When the person who has died is a well-known member of the community or a young person taken far too soon, the pavements will become crowded with people wanting to pay their respects and show their support for the family, often numbering into the thousands.

People will still become aware that someone in the community has passed through word of mouth, of course. Anyone who has ever lived in a village or small town – particularly in Ireland! – will know how news travels. But in addition to this, one of the most popular websites in the country these days is rip.ie, where all death notices are posted, and you can search by area. Local radio stations read out death notices at set times to spread the word. Any of the radio stations will verify that it is one of the most important of their services and attracts many listeners, both here and abroad. This service is very effective at letting everyone know when someone has passed, as I found out when my own death was announced . . .

In the early days, we used to phone in the death notices, and then, before email, faxing them became the norm. I always sent in a fax from our funeral home on our headed notepaper. On one particular evening, there had been some delays in finalising the arrangements for the funeral, so we just managed to get the fax in before the deadline for the evening obituary notices. The death notice was acknowledged, but we didn't have time that evening to listen to them being read out. However, I was soon interrupted from whatever task had taken me away from the radio that night when a funeral director rang me.

I picked up the phone and he said, 'Thank God you answered!'

I had no idea what he was talking about. He proceeded to tell me that my death notice had been read out on the radio.

Bedlam followed as the phone rang incessantly. Apparently, the woman reading the notices that evening had inadvertently read out my name from the headed paper, rather than that of the deceased. Having had several phone calls in relation to the error, she immediately went on air to rectify the problem.

I was still answering calls about my own death that evening, but there was relief among the callers when I answered the phone.

MOST PEOPLE don't take much notice of details when attending a funeral, but these matter when you are the person at the centre of arranging one. Time also means nothing in the course of arranging a funeral, as many people are detached from it as they meet with all of the attention a death brings on a house. It is difficult to think of what to do, and to prioritise tasks to be done. Things like picking readings, photos, etc. are done in a complete haze. That is where I step in. I become immersed in helping the grieving people get through. Yes, I feel their deep loss, but helping them helps me to cope too.

Some decisions taken at this time can go on to have wider-reaching consequences, not anticipated when the funeral was being arranged. I am thinking in particular about a woman who had lost her baby in childbirth, and almost lost her own life too. The baby was buried before she was able to leave hospital, and the decision was taken to place the child in the father's family's plot. Everyone was so distraught at the time, they didn't think about where the parents would eventually be buried. There is also a myth that a baby can't be put into an empty grave, which can lead to some wrong decisions being made, but this is not true.

This decision bothered the mother of the baby for years afterwards, as she really wanted the baby to be buried with her and her husband. She hadn't known it was possible to move her child's remains but I explained that it was, so we got the paperwork required in order to exhume the baby, and we laid her to rest where her mother wanted.

The most challenging funerals, both emotionally and professionally, are those when someone was so full of life has been ripped suddenly from their family and community without warning. There is an atmosphere of shock and grief, and it is a terrible cross to bear. These funerals are usually attended by huge numbers of mourners, as people come from near and far to support the grieving family. I have witnessed, on numerous occasions, long, never-ending lines of people, waiting solemnly to say a final goodbye to the deceased person and offer their deepest sympathy to the family.

There is always a lot to think about when this many people attend a funeral. In these sorts of circumstances in particular, a lot of planning and coordination is involved in making sure that the day goes smoothly, enabling the bereaved to focus completely on the ritual. We liaise with leaders from each group involved in forming the guard of honour for the hearse – for example, there might be people from the deceased's workplace, or sports club, or church – organising where each group will gather to form their line of respect. There is none of the usual chit-chat, as people are without words, under a cloud of melancholy.

When the deceased is a young person, sometimes groups of teenagers gather, in silent shock, not knowing what to do, needing guidance and support through the process. There is often a feeling that they desperately need to do something, but they have no idea what that should be. In this case, I will talk to them and make suggestions, to see what they respond best to. Sometimes, something as basic as gathering photos and compiling them in a book or slideshow can be a consolation to be shared with all. This can be a solace for the family, helping them to connect with friends of their son or daughter in the empty days following the funeral. Bonds are often formed through these actions, which connect people for the rest of their lives.

Funerals of young people lead to terrible upset in a community, and people come to support their family. Families often need some extra time alone with the deceased following all of this. Great care has to be taken to ensure that the bereaved are looked after at all times, and that they don't get lost in the crowd as the funeral cortège slowly makes its way along the road. When my wife Aileen's mother died, there was a huge crowd outside the church after the service. The family members were individually swamped with people wanting to offer their sympathy. Aileen felt overwhelmed, but luckily a friend brought her to one side to give her some space. I know how easy it can be to end up at the back of the crowd in such situations, when everyone wants to tell you how sorry they are, leaving you separated from family and in the wrong place when the time comes to go to the cemetery. So, as I or my team often do when lots of people turn out, I went to find Aileen and escort her through the crowd to make sure she was at the front behind the hearse carrying her mother.

It is also important to manage parking, so that the cars of the bereaved don't get blocked in unintentionally, holding them up and causing unnecessary stress. If you have not seen a large crowd turn out for a funeral in an Irish town or village, this might not sound like a major consideration, but it really can be a real headache, particularly when it comes to making sure everything runs on time. On one occasion, the president was in attendance at a funeral and actually got blocked in this way. In fairness, a very embarrassed driver removed their car promptly, but they first had to be found in the crowd.

My hearses are a dark silver colour, rather than black. While black is associated with death and is the chosen colour for many funeral directors, I believe in the notion of celebrating a person's life, and so the lighter colour feels more appropriate to me personally.

An old funeral director once told me that you should never reverse a hearse when there's a deceased person in the back, as it was believed to bring bad luck to the funeral director. I have often thought about that one, and found myself thinking twice about turning the hearse with a deceased person in it, but it is unavoidable at a lot of churches, as you have to line up the hearse at the church door in order to take the coffin out of it. It is also necessary to reverse the hearse in a cemetery with narrow paths. I guess he was working in an area where he could drive forward on all occasions. Lucky for him!

What is important, though, is to carry the coffin the right way, with the deceased facing in the right direction. I once asked an older funeral director about this, and his explanation was that you don't walk backwards in and out of buildings in life, so you shouldn't do it in death either. Therefore, a coffin should be carried feet first, so that if the person was to get up and walk, they would be headed in the right direction. In the church, the coffin should be placed feet closest to the altar, so the deceased is facing the altar. The only exception is for the clergy. It is believed that they should always face the people they have served. However, this tradition doesn't apply to the way they are buried, or the way they are brought in the hearse. It's interesting which of the traditions continue and which we change or forget.

Interestingly, while we might think that it would always have been the men who carried the coffin, when it came to the time to remove the deceased from the house, the women of the family traditionally carried the coffin to the door of the house, where the men would take over and carry the coffin to the hearse. I remember seeing this often when I was a teenager working for my father. These traditions were kept where circumstances permitted.

Nowadays, it is different. I see a mix of people wanting to carry the coffin at different stages. The bereaved decide among themselves and ask people, regardless of gender, if they would like to be involved in this. It is then my job to assess who is going to be involved at different times, grouping people by their height, as it is very important to ensure that the coffin is carried respectfully, keeping it level throughout. If the funeral director isn't paying attention to this, the coffin can end up being carried in a most undignified way!

I remember one evening, a coffin was being carried into a local church by the family members. The priest was saying the prayers at the door of the church before the coffin was brought in. He wasn't used to the aspersorium and aspergilium – the vessel for holding holy water and the implement used to sprinkle it – in that church. As he read the prayers from his prayer book, he reached for the aspergilium, not realising that this particular one shot out large amounts of water. He shook it rhythmically as he read the prayers, dipping it in the aspersorium a few times to re-wet it, unaware that he was completely drenching the men that were carrying the coffin. One man got a full splash straight into the face. The nervous tension of the men, doing their best to bring the coffin to the church with great dignity and sadness, was suddenly exchanged for them trying to keep serious faces in the midst of a sad occasion, as they tried to hold back their laughter at what had just happened.

Nowadays, the bereaved may opt to place the coffin on a trolley and the people who might otherwise carry it walk alongside as it is taken back to the hearse after the funeral service. This way, wheelchair users, and others who would like be fully involved but who would otherwise not be able, can take part in this stage of the funeral, which holds a lot of meaning for the bereaved, as time with their loved one is quickly running out.

Over the years, I have had many requests to place items in the coffin, from newspapers and reading glasses, to letters from grandchildren and handbags, and, yes, sometimes even mobile phones in more recent times. Watches were common too. I was once asked to place a sword in a coffin, so that the deceased would be able to fight off any bad spirits. Many widowed persons would be buried with their wedding ring still on to display their loyalty to their partner. I have also been asked to put pet ashes in along with their owner in the coffin, at the owner's request.

Death is a very personal thing, so while putting such items in the coffin might seem ridiculous to some, it is the meaning that they hold for the deceased (if they had indicated such wishes before their death) or the bereaved, or both, that is important. Sometimes, in times of grief, when we are bereft and have a terrible void in our lives, it is these small things that can bring us some comfort, helping us to get through the darkest days.

There was a time when the grave was filled in while the bereaved stood and watched. This is still traditional in some places. One might wonder why the grave had to be filled in so soon. One explanation goes back to times when graves were raided for any jewellery that had been buried with the deceased.

In areas like Dublin, medical colleges needed cadavers for the purpose of teaching student doctors and nurses. At the beginning of the 1800s, in the early days of modern medicine, there was a shortage of bodies for teaching and study, and money was offered for any that were donated. This led to the gruesome and terrible practice of raiding graves to remove the deceased from their coffins and sell them to the colleges.

Nowadays – as graverobbing is fortunately a thing of the past! – a grave is often covered with artificial grass mats adorned with some wreaths after the coffin has been lowered, and the gravediggers wait until the bereaved have left before filling in the grave.

JUST AS I DON'T have black hearses, I don't wear black when I am funeral directing. Although many funeral directors do choose to wear a black suit and black tie or scarf (for ladies), this never made sense to me. Traditionally, only the mourners, those closest to the deceased, wore black and the funeral director is not a mourner. Perhaps some thought it appropriate to distinguish themselves from the public, who would wear their Sunday best but not black, but I have often heard of a funeral director being unwittingly sympathised with at funerals by people who have come from outside of the area. I do, of course, take great care in what I wear, as a mark of professionalism and respect – though this has not always been without incident!

One evening, Aileen arrived at the funeral home. As she parked the car, she noticed a man going towards the building carrying a suit. She assumed that he must be part of the bereaved group that had just gone into the funeral home ahead of him. She approached him to see if he needed any help, and the man asked after me with a particularly West of Ireland expression, saying, 'Is he there himself?'

'No, but I can take the suit off you, if you like,' was her reply.

She asked if he thought the suit would fit 'him', meaning the deceased. It's a common problem that people bring in clothes that the person had not worn for many years in life.

Puzzled at the question, the man replied, 'It should fit him; I measured him well.'

Aileen was completely baffled, as she had never heard of anyone taking a measuring tape to the deceased to see if their suit would fit. This was unusually thorough.

But had he worn the suit recently, she persisted.

Getting a little impatient at this stage, the man replied, 'He has not worn it at all yet!'

She asked him what his name was, and he told her it was Packie.

What a bizarre situation, thought Aileen. Why on earth would this Packie bring in a suit for a deceased person that they had never worn? Aileen decided that it was best not to ask any more questions. She instead assured him that she would look after the suit, and proceeded to walk towards the funeral home door. The man didn't follow her as she had thought he would, but perhaps he had to go and do something else pertaining to the funeral.

So she brought in the suit and informed me that she had just hung up it up ready to put on the deceased man.

I looked at her and asked, 'What man?'

The deceased was a lady.

I asked Aileen who had left the suit and she told me that it had been brought in by a man called Packie. I immediately began to laugh. Packie Ward was a well-known tailor in Sligo – though clearly not to Aileen. He had even made a suit for my father when he started out as an undertaker. My father was a short man, and getting a suit to fit wasn't an easy task. The suit Packie just left was one he had tailored for me!

Aileen patiently waited for me to stop laughing to fill her in on what was so funny.

Later that evening, I got a phone call from Packie Ward, eager to know if I liked the new suit that he had just finished for me. He was in stitches when he heard about the mix-up. A very confusing conversation for all involved suddenly became clear!

I wore that suit for some years and it served me well. It managed to avoid the fate of another, far more unfortunate item of my work attire.

It is normal to hang up the clothes for the deceased in the mortuary, so they are convenient to reach when it comes to dressing the deceased person. And this was exactly where the man who was diligently assisting me with the embalming process one evening had hung up the dead man's suit of clothes. Right next to my own new suit jacket.

We reached the point where I was fixing the man's tie. His suit jacket would be put on him next. It is not unusual for us to have to cut a jacket up the centre back seam to ensure that it fits the deceased comfortably. My assistant took down the jacket, and it was clear to him that it was a little too small for the man we were dressing. He carefully cut up the centre of the back of the jacket before handing it to me. We proceeded to position it on the man, when, all of a sudden, I noticed that it was different to the pants we had put on him. At first, I thought that we had been given a jacket and pants instead of a suit, but, as I fixed the jacket, I noticed my pen in the pocket. To my horror, I quickly realised that it was the jacket of my new suit! My assistant realised his mistake and legged it, immediately disappearing from the mortuary.

I then put the proper jacket on the deceased, but I was without my full suit for the evening's visitation and instead had to wear my overcoat throughout.

Needless to say, my assistant and I kept well clear of each other that evening, but we were able to laugh about the mishap eventually – once I got over the loss of my lovely new suit.

'The Last Man to Let You Down'

THE STORY OF THE mix-up with the suit jacket still comes up from time to time, perhaps when a suit is dropped off for someone in our care. It serves to lighten the mood and reminds us that there is a place for humour even amid the serious work we do and the level of respect and dedication it requires. It's similar to how moments of humour can arise among mourners when they recall something funny the deceased once said or did, and, for a moment, everything feels slightly more bearable. This can be important.

People often ask me how I cope with being surrounded by death on a daily basis. It is not easy, but the fulfilment of helping others is a source of great strength for me. I focus on the chosen funeral ritual and do my best to ensure that this goes as smoothly as possible. I try to connect with the bereaved and sense their individual preferences, pre-empting their needs, enabling me to add small details that make a difference for them. I empathise with families and their grief, but also have to be professional in my work, as it is me that they depend on to look after them as they navigate this difficult and unknown territory.

There are times, however, that I get really upset in the course of my work. Sudden deaths, suicides, deaths of close friends and family all affect me deeply. I am especially saddened when the death has circumstances that make me reflect on my own life. I have witnessed parents bury their sons and daughters, and it is extremely difficult not to be affected by this when you come home to your own family. Sometimes there is guilt in knowing that you have been the lucky one this time and have the privilege of more time with your family. I look at my daughters and cannot conceive of my pain if anything happened to them, but I know from my work that this can never be guaranteed. The constant lesson from this is to make the most of every day, with those whom you love, as it could, in an instant, be the last.

I know that I cannot live my live in the grief of others, but it is hard to avoid sometimes. I find talking in confidence to fellow professionals whom I trust is a huge help to me in coping with the pain that I witness on a daily basis.

Tragic deaths often prey on my mind for a long time afterwards. I have spent long nights in the mortuary doing my best to ease the blow to the bereaved of seeing a very disturbing sight. My mind is preoccupied with figuring out the best way to do this. At times like this, it is hard to sleep. I am lucky to have the support of my wife and family, who always help me through these times. I also find prayer and spiritual connections, with the deceased and other deceased people whom I was close to in this life, help me on difficult days.

In the funeral home, members of staff are a huge support to each other. We work together to do our best. Those trips in the hearse can often be a place where supportive conversations take place, as we know that what is shared in the hearse, in the company of the deceased, stays in the hearse. We are human too, and cannot avoid the pain of death completely.

Death comes to all of us at some stage, but the most difficult to accept is the death of a child through illness or through tragic circumstances. I have had the arduous task of laying out little children following death. We don't expect a child's life to end after a few short years, and yet many parents have had to endure the terrible pain of this.

This is hard to take, and poses all kinds of religious and philosophical questions for me. Why is this happening? Why must these parents go through such unbearable grief? How can the rest of us try to support them through such tragedy?

Some of these parents, due to ongoing illness or issues their child had had since birth, will have had close calls on several occasions throughout the child's life, and will have felt the impending fear and pain of death. And yet, even though their child may have been sick for many years, the finality of death is as painful for them as a sudden death – for how can anyone really prepare for the loss of a child?

I have also met parents who believed that they had a healthy child, only to subsequently discover that they are on a journey of limited time with that precious little person. These parents have described their brave children to me, and how they endured terrible pain with dignity and little complaint.

I once received a phone call quite late at night from a distraught father, telling me that his child had passed. He and his wife had spent the previous few years travelling to the children's hospital for treatments. I understood that this child was very special and had carried her illness with great dignity. Her parents wanted me to look after the funeral and arranged to come to me in the funeral home.

That night, I opened the door of the funeral home to a mammy and daddy, cradling their seven-year-old, swathed in her favourite blankie. I felt a deep sense of responsibility as I was entrusted with the care of this little person, in preparing her for her final stay at home with her parents, little brothers, family and friends.

My own daughters were around the same age as the little girl at that time. I told them that the little girl's parents had told me that she liked to say her prayers in a particular place that was special to her. They always referred to her afterwards as they passed that place, remembering it was her special place, and we would always say a prayer for her and her family.

The bereaved often have no idea of all of the spiritual support they get in their times of great sadness through the prayers of others. Kindness is something that is offered in abundance to the bereaved here in Ireland. Long may that continue, as we all need support in times of grief, and that support might not always be easy to see.

Whenever I have had to look after the funeral of a child who has been involved in a tragic accident involving a car, the final lines from Seamus Heaney's 'Mid-Term Break' come to mind, which describe a young boy who has been knocked over by a car and killed. The small size of the coffin is shown by the final line – 'a foot for every year'.

I have looked after children killed as they were passengers or because they unwittingly ran out in front of a car without looking, or were struck by a driver who didn't see them. The tragedy of this is terrible and the pain for all is unbearable. I have even known of deeply sad cases where a parent has been the unfortunate driver, unaware that their little child had followed them out of the house. There are no words that can console parents who have lost children in this way. Sometimes, one can only help by doing practical things. Just being present and sharing memories as they come to mind can be a big help, but it is also important to give these numbed parents space to process the unbearable tragedy that has just happened, as they face the formidable task of laying their child to rest. When something this terrible has happened, I have always seen communities step in and do everything they can to offer support.

It is even more harrowing when the death has not been accidental but has been as a result of the deliberate actions of another. I remember vividly one little toddler who had suffered at the hands of an adult, leading to his death. I knew by his wounds what this child had suffered prior to his death. It is incomprehensible to me that an adult could hurt an innocent child, let alone be responsible for their death. This was a very difficult case to deal with.

I have buried mothers with their babies in their arms, who died through tragic or accidental circumstances. I have also witnessed little children play around the coffin of a parent and kiss Mammy or Daddy goodbye, as the remaining parent holds them up to the coffin, knowing that they may not remember their parent in years to come.

All of these funerals affect me in different ways, and one cannot avoid the pain felt by those closest to children who die through their weeping, wailing cries.

I am proud of my role in the community and have always carried it out with utmost dignity. It is, of course, a great honour that so many people trust me with their loved ones as they prepare to say their final goodbyes. I wouldn't change that for the world, but because of people's complicated and sometimes fearful attitudes towards death, being widely recognised as a funeral director when I am out and about and not at work does bring with it some challenges and difficulties that I don't think people are necessarily aware of.

For example, throughout my life as a funeral director, I have often been the source of well-meaning jokes. I'm often referred to as the 'planter' or 'the last man to let you down'. I've been asked if I've 'stuffed' anyone today. I have been introduced as 'the best boxer in town', usually followed by a question like 'Did you box anyone today?' – meaning did I put anyone in a coffin.

I have a sense of humour, but these jokes go stale after a few times – never mind after hearing them over and over again over the years.

I remember being in a busy restaurant one evening with my daughter Eithne when she was young. I knew most of the people in the restaurant. As we were being brought to our table, people were nodding at me, asking 'Have you the tape with you?' As we sat down, a group at the table beside us joked, 'Don't be looking over here, because you will only be measuring us up!' Eithne didn't understand that they were referring to being measured for a coffin and asked, 'Dad, what do they mean?' I had to explain to her over dinner that they were only poking fun, and that it comes with the job.

Aileen and I went into a pub for a few drinks after dinner one night. There were five or six lads sitting at the bar counter, and they started joking with me as I entered the pub, saying, 'Look who's in now, we better be careful!' and asking the usual type of questions.

What people making jokes like this in a public place don't think about is that there may well be people around them who are very recently bereaved, or even who may have been to see me that very week because they have lost a loved one. In those situations, when I know that recently bereaved people are nearby and can probably hear every word, I have sometimes wished that the ground would swallow me up. I never want people to think that I would joke about their loved one behind their backs. It's not who I am. But I can't say anything to the jokers to shut them up as I would never discuss my work in this way, so I have often stood there mortified, trying to quickly change the subject.

On one occasion, the son of a man had all of his friends on standby as his father lay on his death bed. He summoned them on several occasions over the course of a week to come, after the doctor, nurse, or even the priest had visited the house, thinking his father was about to take his last breath. Each time, the loyal friends would arrive to sympathise with the family, only to discover that the man was still alive. Eventually, when the man did pass, the son once again rang the old reliables to say, 'Daddy is dead.' After having come three different times at this stage, each time finding the man still alive, they asked how he knew for sure that his daddy was dead this time. His answer was, ''Cause David McGowan is here!' That was the certification of death!

So is it any wonder that I have sometimes been referred to as Dr Death or the Grim Reaper? In my working life, my presence signifies a death. My job carries a stigma.

But I have secretly craved another identity, wanting to be able to switch roles when I wasn't working. I wanted to be able to walk into a restaurant and not be the trigger of grief and thoughts of funerals in the minds of people greeting me. So I often wondered if I could change my profile in some way. Could I ever be known for a different reason, one that was connected with fun and joy instead of pain and death? I pondered this for many years.

Back when I worked in the bar in Easkey, I always enjoyed meeting tourists who were attracted to our picturesque county of Sligo, with its varied coastline and interesting people. Yet I have often felt that, because of our location in the extreme west of Sligo, we get forgotten in the big picture of tourism in Ireland. In the past, areas near the six counties in Northern Ireland were often avoided by foreign tourists due to the Troubles there; it was like the whole area was cut off the map for visitors. I thought we were something of an undiscovered area with lots of potential, and one thing we needed was more accommodation in the area for tourists.

In 2013, I was fortunate enough to be contacted by a family selling a site in Enniscrone. It was perfect for the development of tourist accommodation, and Enniscrone is certainly a hidden gem in terms of Irish holiday resorts. Although I was very busy at the time with my funeral business, the offer set off lots of ideas and I decided to purchase the site.

The following year saw the development of the Wild Atlantic Way by Fáilte Ireland, the national authority for promoting tourism. This was a mapped, signed route for tourists to follow around the west coast of Ireland, from Kinsale in West Cork, all the way to Malin Head in County Donegal – a total of 2,500 km. Enniscrone was listed as a discovery point on the route. Ten million euros were invested in the route, and it had massive potential to bring more visitors and jobs in the tourism sector to rural communities right along the western seaboard. When I noticed an increase in foreign number plates on the roads in our area that summer, I knew that the Wild Atlantic Way was going to be a success.

I had decided by this point that I wanted to offer something that was different and quirky, to bring a sense of fun and curiosity to the area. I researched a lot of designs of accommodation units, and then discovered the concept of glamping, which was evolving at that time. I liked that idea and its potential for a variety of pods as opposed to just one style of unit throughout the site. Then one day, I had a brainwave. How about turning modes of transport into accommodation? I was fascinated by the work of architects like George Clarke, and projects that converted all kinds of small spaces into permanent or temporary living spaces, and I began to see potential for living spaces in every mode of transport around me.

That was fun, but soon the idea grew, and I started to investigate the idea of purchasing a decommissioned Boeing 767 and bringing it to the site . . . somehow! Aileen and my daughters, Mary, Bríd and Eithne, could have thought I'd lost the plot, but they understood what I was trying to do and were extremely supportive throughout the whole process. With a certain amount of serendipity, I had discovered that a plane had been abandoned at Shannon airport – not too far away – by a Russian company that had gone into liquidation. They were keen to get rid of it.

After much work with my architect and engineer, the planning application was submitted for the glamping site in 2015. With planning permission approved and an agreement to purchase the decommissioned plane, which had been stripped of all its seats and inner workings, the whole idea was quickly becoming a reality. However, moving the plane was almost unimaginable – a 767 is 48 metres long, so almost the length of an Olympic-sized swimming pool – and it was going to be a huge challenge to overcome.

The *Anton Savage Show* on national radio station Today FM got wind of the project, and Anton began regularly chatting to me on his show, meaning the whole thing became a talking point across the entire country. It was obviously making people smile, as the story gained more and more momentum and was reported worldwide on international news channels.

Shannon Airport is about 200 km by road from Enniscrone – not that it would ever be possible to move something that big by road! A plan was hatched to bring it by floating it on a barge along the Shannon estuary and towing it along the Atlantic coast. Unsurprisingly, this mammoth task, taking two days, involved huge support – from airport staff, the Gardaí, the local community council in Enniscrone, teams of first responders, engineers and many, many more. I could never have envisaged the overwhelming assistance and encouragement I was to get from people from all walks of life. It was the *meitheal* in the truest sense of the word.

The mad nature of the whole idea of floating a Boeing 767 on the sea was almost the most important part of the project. The weather was amazing when we did it – the plane just made it ashore before the usual Atlantic swells picked up – and the video footage and photographs were fantastic. I heard that someone who lived in north-west

Mayo hadn't heard about the transition, and on opening their curtains that morning, they saw a huge plane in the middle of their usual vista of the wild Atlantic. They realised what was going on when they went to the shore to find a crowd of people taking photos and cheering it on.

Thousands flocked to Enniscrone for what was a very joyous occasion. I received massive support from everyone. As the plane waited for the tide to be right to land it on the beach, flares were set off. These were in memory of those who had perished in the waters near Enniscrone and at other locations around the coast. That was a very poignant moment.

The night before the plane came, the 'Darkness to Light' walk took place, which raises funds for Pieta House, a charity aimed at preventing suicide and self-harm. Many people had been up all night for that, and then waited to see the plane delivered to the site in the early hours of the next morning.

Without seeking any publicity, my plans for the glamping site and the aeroplane had quickly become my new identity in the public eye. I was no longer known as the funeral director or undertaker, bringing thoughts of sadness, but instead there was fun everywhere I went. No one asked if I had my measuring tape with me; I was being stopped and asked if I was the man who brought the plane to Enniscrone. I had no intention of leaving behind my funeral-directing vocation, but this project had given me what I wanted – an alter ego, allowing me to escape life among the dead for periods of time.

Strangely enough, though, there was some crossover between these two worlds. We couldn't go anywhere without meeting people who wanted to talk about the plane, and I was asked to do some talks on the subject. I enjoyed this. I found it very fulfilling spending time with people from all walks of life. Included in this were some people who were terminally ill. The whole mad concept of the plane had brought joy to their day, while knowing that I was a funeral director opened up a way for them to talk about their mortality.

Once the plane was in situ in Enniscrone, I had numerous calls from people who wanted to visit the site. I had now become a tour guide as well! It was sad at times, when people came who were in the final stages of a terminal illness. But it was always uplifting to know that they had enjoyed the trip. I enjoyed showing young people of all abilities around the site. Some of the most thought-provoking questions came from these young people, and one young lad knew absolutely everything there was to know about Boeing 767 planes!

It had become so much more than the original idea for a glamping site, taking on a whole new agenda, bringing joy in a most unexpected way.

Aileen and I decided that this site would go on to prioritise inclusion. Things like natural sensory areas throughout, quiet places to escape to and interesting things to investigate will hopefully make holidaying more enjoyable and accepting of neurodiversity. We want it to be accessible for anyone with any physical or intellectual challenge, and those with mobility issues.

This, of course, will mean fitting in fewer accommodation pods, which makes pitching the concept to investors harder, as they care little for a vision of inclusion and are not impressed unless you pack as many units in as possible. At this stage, we believe in holding firm to our vision, and hope that some day after you read this book, the glamping site will be a reality and you will be able to come and stay.

In the meantime, I realise that moving that plane inspired and motivated a lot of people. It brought attention to the area we live in. It sent out the message that if you surround yourself with good people, you can make things happen. Most of all, it had changed other people's perceptions of me, and I was no longer connected with death alone in the minds of the public.

Unexplained Happenings

I WAS IN THE MORTUARY one day with a woman in her late forties. I had all but finished getting her ready and had settled her into her coffin. All that was left was to do were her make-up and her hair. I have often been complimented on my work in these areas, and I had never before had any issues with cosmetics. However, this lady was to prove different to any other person I had put cosmetics on. Her skin blatantly rejected any cosmetics, and I repeatedly had to remove the make-up and start again.

I couldn't understand it at all. Could the cosmetics that I was using somehow have been a bad batch? I opened a brand new bottle, but, alas, I had the same result. Even the lipstick was not staying on her lips and was being repelled in the same way that emulsion paint is resisted on a wall where a child has been colouring with a wax crayon.

It was now past 5pm, when the woman was expected back at her home for the wake. Her daughters rang to know if we were on the way, as some neighbours had gathered and wanted to form a guard of honour at the house for her. I decided to give up on the make-up and have another try at getting it right when I reached the house, though I didn't know how I was going to explain this unfinished task to the family, especially her daughters. But honesty is always the best policy and I planned on telling them exactly what was going on with their mother's make-up, and that I would try again later.

When we set up the coffin, her daughters came into the room immediately, desperately wanting to see their mother. It was their time in her presence, so I made myself scarce and went to the kitchen, though without having had a chance to explain to them about their mother's make-up. In the kitchen, I was presented with a cup of tea and a carefully made sandwich.

Soon, I could hear the daughters coming out of the room where their mother was to look for me. I was sure that I was in for a bout of complaint. Instead, each daughter gave me a big hug. They told me that she looked so much like herself. They were particularly grateful to me for not using make-up on her. They told me that they had forgotten to tell me that their mother had hated wearing make-up and never wore it, even on special occasions. They said that she had joked with them in the lead-up to her death, telling them that she would come back to haunt them if they put any make-up on her when she died.

I guess she got her wishes and I was the facilitator of that, even though the situation was completely out of my control.

Many unusual things like this have happened in the years I have been working as a funeral director. There have been times when something odd happening has led to me doing things in a different way, and it has turned out that this was appropriate for the deceased or what they would have wanted, though I didn't know that at the time. Some may justly think that it could be my imagination running away with me, that it is total coincidence; however, I am convinced that there are good reasons for these things happening.

I am of the belief that there is a spiritual presence when I work with the deceased. I believe that I help that spirit in parting with the body that represented them in life, that I have a role in easing the deceased away from those they loved and were loved by. On many occasions, I have not felt alone in the presence of the deceased. Sometimes that feeling gives me a sense of peace and contentment. Sometimes I sense an unsettled feeling.

There may be changes over the years in how Irish people practise their faith, but in my experience of working with the bereaved, faith has never been stronger. Faith presents itself in many different ways; for some, it involves participation in a group practice, and for others it is very individual. There are many beliefs around death that come from religion or simply personal belief and experience. I respect the beliefs of others. If you believe that when we die, we immediately cease to exist, then that is entirely your right. All I can do is tell you about some of the strange experiences I have had in the course of my working life. I don't pretend to know what was happening.

I ONCE HAD a very unusual experience when working with a deceased healer. She was left-handed and had always used this hand to touch her patients. As I worked through the embalming process, I noticed problems arising with the left hand. At first, it did not appear to be responding to the embalming. I massaged it gently as I normally would when there's an area not responding to the injection. However, it turned strange colours and swelled slightly. Some fluid appeared on the hand, but there was no cut or any place it could have come from. I kept a nervous watch on it throughout, and that hand continued to be unusual for the entire repose. I have never witnessed anything like it before or since. The only thing that makes sense to me is that the hand in question was special, and had in life absorbed the affliction of many throughout a lifetime, and now somehow seemed to be purging the bad. I can't explain this other than through speculation of this kind.

There have also often been times when strange things have happened with the hearse on its travels in the course of a funeral. One such event happened very early on after

I opened up the funeral home in Ballina. I could only afford a second-hand hearse at the time, but it was in good working order and always proved reliable, except for on one occasion.

In our town, it is customary for people to walk behind the hearse as a mark of respect. We were making our way from the funeral home to the cathedral, and I was walking ahead of the hearse, as I usually did. I had nearly crossed the bridge over the Moy when I glanced back to discover that the hearse was stopped just about halfway over the bridge.

A hearse breaking down is a funeral director's worst nightmare. It was particularly bad for me at the time, as my business was in its early years and at that stage you want everything to be right. So I was really embarrassed as I made my way back to the hearse on the bridge, where a guard of honour from the local sports club stood on either side of the road. I spoke briefly to the driver, who told me that the hearse had just cut out and wouldn't restart. He too was embarrassed and thought that he might have done something wrong. But there wasn't any time for investigations; all I knew was that I had to get the funeral to the cathedral, which was only a short distance away. My first thought was to carry the coffin from that spot, but I quickly thought that perhaps a little push might get the hearse to start up again as it rolled down the slope from the middle of the bridge. So I asked the members of the guard of honour standing closest on either side to place their hands on the hearse and to give it a little push. I was so relieved when the hearse started up again.

The hearse gave no other trouble, and the rest of that funeral went smoothly. I took the vehicle to the garage afterwards to have it checked, and the mechanics could find nothing wrong with it at all. They had no explanation for what had happened.

I dreaded meeting the family again after the funeral, and went over my apology to them for what had happened over and over again in my mind. I had wanted everything to be perfect for them, and felt that I had let them down. But when I eventually met them when they came into the funeral home a few weeks after the funeral, I was shocked at what they told me. Instead of a reprimand for the hearse stopping on the way to the cathedral, they were grateful to me!

The man's son proceeded to tell me that his dad had often told him that he loved to look down at the river from the bridge to his favourite spot, the place where he had loved to go fishing in the river. He had often fished with his dad there in the past. He had forgotten about his dad telling him that when he died, he wanted the hearse to stop in the middle of the bridge on his final journey. He couldn't believe it when I had stopped the hearse in the exact spot, and had assumed that someone had told me prior to the funeral, or that it was a member of the guard of honour on the bridge.

I couldn't pretend that I had stopped the hearse on purpose. I told him the truth about the hearse just stopping for no apparent reason. We both laughed and figured that his dad had orchestrated a final stop to enable everyone to experience his place on the river. The family had got a great sense of peace from that delay on the bridge, and it was even more comforting for them to discover that it wasn't pre-planned by me or my staff. They even left a gift for us, which was very much appreciated at the time.

That was far from my only experience of the wishes or preferences of the dead being observed, apparently without the intercession of the living.

When I bring a deceased person back to their or their relative's house for a wake, I usually quickly survey the house for the best room to place the coffin in. I take into account the route to the room from the external door, as houses are not designed with a wake in mind. Entry and exit points are important too, as large crowds may need to be moved through the house when the wake is at its busiest. Safety is really important, and people have to be able to go through the house comfortably, in an orderly fashion.

On one particular occasion, I had completed my checks and chosen the sitting room as my preferred location for the deceased to rest in his coffin. The family confirmed that they agreed with my choice. So I organised a group to carry in the coffin and, once inside the house, we placed it on a trolley and wheeled it into the sitting room. There were a few options for where we could place the coffin, but in the domestic setting, placing it near a wall makes maximum use of the space available, making it easier to allow people to get in and out of the room.

We asked the family to step out for a few moments while we removed the lid and fixed the man in his coffin. When all was ready, we left the room so the family of the man could have some private time with him before others were allowed in to sympathise.

I gently closed the door behind me and, as I was speaking to the man's daughter, I heard a loud bang from the room. My colleague and I looked at each other and immediately returned to the room. There we discovered that a picture had fallen off the wall, on the opposite side of the room to where we had placed the coffin. The deceased's wife entered the room, having heard the bang too. She started to laugh. She told us that, for the past thirty years, he had said he didn't like that picture. She loved it, and the picture had stayed in the exact same place all that time. She said that he always joked about not sitting opposite that picture, and that 'her side' of the room was the one with the fine view of her *lovely* picture. She told me that I had placed the coffin on her side of the room, and it looked like he was not going to be forced to look at the picture one last time.

We granted his wish and moved him to 'his' side of the room. The funeral proceeded without any further unusual events after that.

Sometimes, it's the little things that make a difference, even in death!

I'm certainly not the only person who has experienced strange, unexplained incidents at funerals. My three daughters are qualified embalmers and have all worked in the business at different times. Bríd had a really stressful experience with one funeral, which required the deceased to be repatriated from London.

There are two ways that we can do this. One is to send funeral directors over to the UK in a hearse to collect the deceased from where they are being kept. This journey involves travelling on the ferry with the hearse. The alternative is to employ a funeral director in the other country to bring the coffin to the airport. We then take care of everything once the coffin arrives in Ireland by air. We work with the bereaved in choosing the most suitable way.

In the case of this funeral, my daughter Bríd, who manages the Foley and McGowan's Funeral Home in Sligo, had organised a hearse to travel to London for the deceased lady, and had organised the funeral Mass on this end. Everything was in place and the bereaved had booked their flights to Ireland, returning to the UK the day after the funeral. All was going perfectly to plan until Bríd received a call from two very concerned funeral directors on the M25. Just outside London, traffic on the motorway had come to a complete standstill. They had lost almost an hour, which with a ferry to catch wasn't good. They didn't think that they would get to the ferry in time, and were placing Bríd on standby to postpone the funeral for a day.

This is a nightmare scenario for a funeral director. The implications of such changes to arrangements have a knock-on effect across the board. She called the family, preparing them for the unavoidable changes that might have to be made. They were not impressed, and nor were the other people who were to be involved in the funeral. The church had a wedding booked in the following day; the soloist was not available either. The gravediggers were concerned that, having prepared the grave, the inclement weather would lead to problems with it, should there be a delay. The hotel looking after the catering for the funeral party had no availability the following day, as they had been booked for the same wedding as was taking place in the church.

It was a very worrying scenario from behind the scenes, not to mention for the two who were literally stuck on the M25, with the prospect of having to stay overnight in Holyhead. What were they going to do with the hearse – or, more importantly, with the deceased?

All was resolved, however, when a phone call came in from the hearse on the M25. Mercifully, the traffic had started to move again. As the hearse approached the point of the blockage, they expected to see the carnage of a terrible accident. But that wasn't the cause of the delay. Instead, a herd of goats was being driven by a woman and some volunteers who had left their cars to help. The police were also involved. They had finally managed to coax them back to the gap in the hedge through which they had escaped onto the motorway, and secured the gap to prevent further havoc.

Greatly relieved, Bríd contacted the family of the deceased woman to tell them that the funeral could go ahead as planned. They were still upset and wanted to know what had caused the delay in the first place. So Bríd explained to them that goats had managed to escape onto the motorway, and they hadn't been very cooperative in returning to their pasture.

She could hear the woman telling the others in the room about the cause of the delay, followed by an outburst of laughter from the room. The person who had taken the call was among the loudest laughing. When the lady got herself composed a little bit, she proceeded to tell Bríd why they all found this so funny.

Apparently, their aunt had moved to London and had settled there. Deep down, she always wanted to return home to Ireland, but she never got around to moving home. She developed a love of goats and had always wanted to keep some. But, of course, it's not easy to find a house to rent in London if you decide to keep goats, so she had to abandon the idea. Instead, she took every opportunity that came her way to visit any farm that had goats. How bizarre that her funeral was delayed on the M25 because of goats!

Whether or not you believe in any spiritual intervention, you have to admit that this is not a normal everyday occurrence on the M25 and it was, at the very least, an unusual coincidence.

When the hearse arrived back at the funeral home, Bríd and Eithne, our youngest daughter, set about their usual task of fixing the lady in the coffin after the long journey and touching up her make-up.

Eithne likes to have music playing for the deceased. On this occasion, a song by a particular famous singer came on. But the sound became distorted all of a sudden, sounding like a radio that was not tuned in to any frequency. This continued for a few minutes and, just as the girls were about to fix the music, the song came to an end and the sound returned to normal.

Eithne says this often happens when she plays music in the mortuary, and she feels it's the spirit's way of telling her to change the music, which she does.

Later, when they were talking to the relatives of the lady, they told them of the sound going all fuzzy when that particular song came on. They laughed and in chorus said that she had hated that song and the singer too. She always made them switch it off if it came on the TV or radio! So I guess this woman's spirit was very much around for the duration of her funeral, and she had all of her wishes granted in the end, especially those relating to her love of goats!

It can be a lovely thing when unexpected and slightly unusual events bring some light relief to a sad day. For example, there was consternation one day when my phone went missing. In the normal run of things, my phone gets put down if I have to attend to something, and usually turns up very soon. This time was different, however. I knew that I'd had my phone in the breast pocket of my suit just before we closed the coffin. And yet it was nowhere to be found.

I rang Andrew, the funeral director who was driving the hearse, but his phone wasn't connected to the hearse's phone system and he wasn't able to answer it while driving.

The more we searched for my phone, the more convinced we were that it was not on the premises. Then we had a brainwave. Someone suggested using the 'find my iPhone' function. That took a while, because I couldn't remember my password! Aileen was at home and she persevered until she eventually got into the website. She was able to tell me exactly where the phone was. I knew by the location that phone was in the hearse, and also that the funeral party would be stopping to eat before long. We waited in anticipation for a call back from Andrew.

After what seemed like ages, Andrew called one of my daughters. She explained to him that the phone was in the hearse, and that I was worried it was in the coffin. Imagine a phone going off in the middle of the ceremony in the crematorium!

He searched the hearse and called me back; he couldn't find the phone. I racked my brains, trying to retrace my every step after closing the coffin. We already knew the phone was on board, but if it was in the coffin itself, it was going to be a problem.

Andrew went back again, searching the glove compartment, under both seats, in the door pockets, even over the sun visor, but to no avail. Then I thought of the only other place it could possibly be. I had put the trolley into the hearse after we had placed the coffin into it. We had put the trolley into the lower compartment of the hearse. Sure enough, the phone turned up in that compartment. What a relief.

Other funny little things had happened throughout that funeral, and I wondered afterwards if the deceased person was playing tricks on us. In life, he'd had a playful spirit and had never missed an opportunity for some fun when the chance arose.

I HAVE OFTEN HEARD people speak of 'signs' being sent to us from the spiritual world – something that stands out as very unusual. For example, I remember reading about a black butterfly appearing at the funeral of Amy Winehouse as her father did the eulogy. I have also witnessed lone butterflies at funerals.

One could argue, justifiably so, that butterflies are normally around in the summer and autumn, so there is nothing terribly unusual about that. But it is, however, unusual for us, here in the West of Ireland, to see red admiral butterflies in the depths of winter. I have even seen lone butterflies on days when we have been pelted with hailstones. One theory could be that they came out of hibernation early in a church that had been heated up. Let me tell you, I've seen them in pretty cold churches where the heating system isn't working particularly well. You most certainly would not even open the buttons of your coat in some of these places, let alone take it off. It has always puzzled me as to where these lone creatures have come from at such times. It also puzzles me why they tend to move around the coffin and the bereaved at the front of the church. Again, it could be argued that they somehow came with the flowers, but some of these funerals haven't had flowers at all, with donations going to a charity instead.

Feathers are another thing that are often taken as signs of spiritual messages. I have heard people speak of seeing a feather that in some way guided them, and I have had this experience.

I was once looking after the funeral of a relative of my own. The lady had passed peacefully and there had been a beautiful funeral Mass for her. When we got to the cemetery, I was both funeral director and mourner. I led the cortège to the grave and followed the usual procedure with the final prayers at the graveside. When it came to the point at which the coffin was to be lowered into the grave, I was standing at the foot of the coffin as the others held the tapes to lower it into the ground. As they lifted the coffin, I noticed a feather lying on the base of the grave. It was a white feather, about seven centimetres or three inches long. I am pretty certain it wasn't there when we brought the coffin in, as I always scan the grave when I bring a coffin to rest on the planks placed over the grave.

As they lowered the coffin into the grave, the feather floated up towards me. It was a bit like when they reverse play an action in a film. It floated as you would expect it to float when moving in the direction of the ground, but this feather was coming up instead of going down. It continued upwards past my head and disappeared. I looked around for it afterwards, but it wasn't to be seen. I suppose it could have landed anywhere. Although it was a strange sight for me, I also felt a sense of calm and peace come over me, as it disappeared upwards past me. I had a comforting feeling and sensed that her spirit had moved at that particular time and she was content.

I CAN SAY, on the basis of plenty of experience, that pets definitely experience the deaths of their owners in a unique way. I also feel that they have an extra sense that we don't have.

One morning, I was attending to a funeral that was going from the residence of the deceased to the church. In some cases, when the wake is to take place in the deceased's own home, the relatives might ask that the deceased spends the last night in their own bed. This was the case for this funeral.

We arrived at the house the next day with the coffin and began getting the mourners to say their last goodbye. All went as normal, with the lady's husband waiting until last. We closed the door to allow him precious time alone with his late wife. When he emerged from the room, a dog appeared and pushed into the room. The family apologised and attempted to remove the dog, but he was not having any of it. He was a big dog and one wouldn't challenge him lightly. They said he was their mother's dog and that he had been very subdued since her passing, and he wasn't used to large crowds in the house either. I said we should let him into the room for just a minute.

As soon as we let him in, he went straight for the bed and hopped up on it. He rested his paws on the lady's chest and nestled his snout under her chin. He then began to lick her face before resting his head back down on her chest. I tried to move him off her when it was time to start putting her in the coffin. He wasn't budging for me. I didn't persevere. Instead, I asked a member of the family if they could get him to go out. When they beckoned to him, he licked his mistress's hands and face one final time and then quietly crept off the bed and moved out of the room.

We laid the woman in her coffin and proceeded with moving her to the church. On arrival, the priest remarked that I was a few minutes late. That was unusual, as I pride myself with always keeping a funeral to the times agreed, unless of course some unforeseen happening causes a delay. In this case, it was the woman's dog, who was missing his owner terribly and needed to say that last goodbye in his own way. All dog lovers will understand.

We have had dogs over the years, and I really understand when people describe their pet as part of the family. Even though I am used to dogs, I am always wary of them when it comes to anything being wrong with the owner. Likewise, I never take a dog's response for granted in relation to moving a deceased person from their home.

I have seen dogs lie next to and sometimes even under a coffin in the wake house, and it is clear to me that they too are mourning the loss of their owner. They remain loyal, even in death. Like I did with the lady's pet that I just mentioned, I have had to get family members to coax the dog out so that we can begin to close the coffin and bring it to the place where the funeral ceremony will take place. I have been growled at, believe me, and when I see those teeth, I daren't challenge the defensive dog in question.

On several occasions, I have been told later by the bereaved that a cherished pet only lived for a month or two after the owner's death. Such was their dedication that they lost all will to live and stopped eating for their new carer.

A woman called me one night to help her lift her drunk husband upstairs to bed. The man had been on the beer all day and appeared to be asleep, sitting on the chair at the bottom of the stairs. She was cross with him for coming home in that state, as he'd been due home hours before that for a dinner that she had cooked.

When I arrived at the house, the man appeared sound asleep. His dog was on his knee. The dog was very anxious and was barking madly. Every so often, his barking stopped as he licked the man's face. He growled at me when I approached the man, so I stepped back. The man looked pale, but apart from that I wasn't alarmed, as I had often seen him in this state before and he always got up and perked up after a snooze.

The man's wife continued to shake him and was clearly losing patience with him at this stage.

I was in front of the man and his wife was to his side, so perhaps she didn't see what I could see. I noticed his face getting paler, but I was afraid to go any closer as the dog was howling at this stage. I asked her if we should call the doctor, but she said that he would be fine after he got to sleep it off.

I tried approaching him again, but the dog went mad. I wasn't happy about the situation and decided to go outside. I called the doctor, who was a very good friend of mine.

When he arrived, the woman had to bring out the dog so that the doctor could examine her husband. To everyone's horror, the doctor pronounced him dead. He had been dead since before I arrived. I couldn't believe that neither the man's wife nor I had for one minute thought of him passing away. I suppose that the dog created such a fuss that the situation seemed completely mad.

It's not just dogs that show great loyalty when their owner dies; I have seen cats show similar tendencies.

I once laid a woman out in her coffin, positioning it in her favourite place in the kitchen. I set up the crucifix and candles on a little table next to her, and got the shock of my life when I turned back to start fixing the side sheets of the coffin. What did I see curled up at the woman's feet but a black and white cat. I hadn't noticed it sneaking into the coffin.

I called in the son of the woman and asked him if he knew anything about the cat. He threw his eyes up to heaven. 'That cat drives me mad, and Mam used to have her in here the whole time. She used to sit on her knees, and if Mam was working in the kitchen, she would brush by her with her tail in the air, as she rubbed against her legs, purring. She even went up on the worktop at times!'

One of his sisters scolded him, saying that their mother loved that cat. She began petting the cat and rubbing her chin. The cat purred happily. For two days, the cat loyally stayed to watch over her beloved owner. She didn't bother anyone, just stayed curled up at the foot of the coffin.

When the time came for closing the coffin, she would not leave. Eventually, one of the grandchildren managed to coax her out with a treat. The removal from the residence took place without any drama, and the cat stayed out of the way. Or, at least, that's what I'd thought!

As we lead the funeral cortège along the roadway from the house, the funeral car immediately behind the hearse started to flash its lights at me.

I stopped, thinking that I had failed to pause at a location that was important to the deceased. The driver kept flashing the lights. I got out and went back to him, now wondering if someone was ill or if we had forgotten to wait for a family member. He gestured to the hearse and smirked. 'Look where Kitty has landed herself now!' he said.

Sure enough, there was Kitty, perched on the coffin, observing all around her with great pride. She must have slipped into the hearse when the front doors were open.

Poor Kitty was removed promptly by one of the family members and taken into one of the cars. She was not impressed. She had just wanted to stay with her owner for as long as possible.

I have even witnessed a donkey getting really distressed at a wake house. He brayed loudly in a plaintive, eerie cry. He made several attempts to make his way into the front garden of the house where his owner was laid out. I was worried about what he could potentially do when we had to move the coffin to the hearse for the funeral. I feared for the safety of those attending, and also about the potential of him lashing out at the neighbours who were to carry the coffin, in the event of him escaping from the field he was in.

I was to discover that this donkey had been a real pet of the deceased. He was called Hamish, and Hamish was openly showing his grief.

I called a neighbour aside and asked if he ever helped out on the farm there, and if he would be able to do something with Hamish. He laughed at me in disbelief and told me in no uncertain terms that Hamish had a definite mind of his own, and that the only person he ever responded to was the woman who lay in the coffin.

Having failed to find someone to take care of Hamish, I decided to ask one of the family in the house. They said that he wouldn't leave his field and not to worry about him. I nervously trusted their judgement, but from my days of driving my friend P.J.'s donkey cart in Easkey, I knew well what a donkey was capable of, if not happy with a situation.

As the hearse departed the house, I walked ahead of it down the boreen towards the main road. Alongside me was yon donkey, braying away, as he accompanied the hearse on its journey. I'd never heard anything like the wailing of him. He knew for sure that something was wrong, perhaps even that his favourite person in the world was gone.

On another occasion, a young showjumper passed away tragically. A life dedicated to horses ended very suddenly, leaving behind a devastated family and large circle of friends. The family were in a complete state of shock and decided not to travel to Dublin with the hearse to collect the young person.

That journey back from Dublin was very melancholic, as I knew it was going to be really hard for the close-knit family of this talented young man. There was a delay with the traffic ahead and everything slowed down. I noticed that three horses had begun to gallop, full speed, in their field alongside the hearse.

I remarked on them. They were beautiful animals. I had seen horses gallop alongside vehicles, before so there was nothing unusual about that. However, as the traffic came to a complete standstill, the horses did a most unusual thing. They turned to face the hearse and lined up, side by side. I couldn't believe what came next. They lowered their heads to the ground, as if bowing to the coffin in the hearse. A strange yet comforting feeling came over me. I felt connected, in that moment, to this equine gesture of respect, so apt for this young man who was always at his happiest when he was surrounded by horses.

These encounters are valuable stories to be shared with the bereaved, at a time when they are feeling completely lost. I feel it is important to share my experiences with them, as, at the very least, they can bring some tiny consolation in the midst of devastation. I understand that some people don't really get this, but for those of us who do, it can bring great hope in terrible times.

The Funeral Director

IN 2002, GILLIAN MARSH, a film producer, was contemplating the idea of making a documentary on death and funerals in the Irish setting. She had a vision for how it should be, wanting it to be done respectfully. But she couldn't see how to make it happen, not least because she didn't know any funeral directors at the time. She became busy with other work and parked the idea for a while.

In 2009, when Gillian's dad passed away, I was called to look after the funeral. He was from Newbridge, but had died at Gillian's home in Crossmolina. The family had anticipated a few friends wanting to pay their respects when he was brought to the funeral home in Ballina. Not knowing the town and the respect paid to funerals here, and having spent much time in Dublin where this is not the norm, Gillian never imagined the overwhelming support they were to receive from the large crowds that came to be with them that evening.

In the days after Gillian's dad's funeral, I had several conversations with Gillian. The topic that kept coming up was that of making a documentary to allay people's fears around death. She wanted to help people to understand what happens between the time the bereaved entrusts their loved one to the care of the funeral director to the time when they see him or her laid out in a coffin for the funeral. This was reality television, in a sense, but it was not for entertainment. It was to give people an insight into the process and hopefully offer some consolation to those who are grieving the loss of someone very close to them.

I had doubts about the whole thing, but the more Gillian explained her concept to me, the more I felt that this was something that needed to be done. But how?

Over the next few years, we talked many times about how it might be possible. It wasn't going to be straightforward. Some parts would be easy enough, as neither deceased nor bereaved would be needed for filming, but how on earth could we ever ask a bereaved family or a terminally ill person to participate in a documentary, where their grief would be shared with a worldwide audience?

Gillian had a film crew who worked with her regularly. She was prepared to be on standby in order to capture footage at short notice in the event of someone agreeing to participate.

It was all unheard of in the West of Ireland, so plucking up the courage to ask a family if they would be willing to feature in the film project was never going to be easy. How could I be talking to bereaved people one minute about what they wanted for their loved one and then, in the middle of all, ask them about participating in a documentary? I made several funeral arrangements and couldn't ask, as I felt it would be wrong and insensitive of me. I just couldn't do it.

In the meantime, Gillian began filming interviews with me. We were also able to work on general scenes, with staff preparing for funerals, etc. I shared my experiences with her and, as I did so, she was quietly crafting out the documentary in the background.

She continued filming over at least five years. All the while, the missing clips were beckoning us. If we couldn't do these, then the rest of the documentary would be futile.

One solution that we came up with was to get actors to act out a wake in a house, to get us over the problem. All was set up in great detail. Actors prepared for the scene. Even Gillian's mum got involved. Everybody did their best to recreate what a wake in the West of Ireland is really like. I arrived with the hearse and greeted the 'mourners' on my arrival. The footage was good, but I knew in my heart and soul that it wasn't going to be true to everything I had talked about in all of the interviews with Gillian. It wasn't real. It wasn't right. There was our dilemma, leaving the documentary on hold indefinitely.

By 2017, Gillian had been commissioned to do a full-length programme on death for RTÉ. I found myself dodging her calls and visits, as I didn't think I would have a hope of asking anyone to participate. How could I?

Then one day, my path crossed Dougie's. Dougie was a pilot, and he had travelled the world over. He was an amazing man who had lived a life packed full of adventure and achievements. He had recently been dealt the terrible blow of a cancer diagnosis. He was devastated but determined to fight it. However, eventually, he had to try to accept the fact that this disease was not going to let go. There was no cure for his illness, only medication that might help him to manage his pain on this final journey he hadn't signed up for.

Talking to him made me thankful for my health, and made me realise how precious every day of good health is. Many of us get caught up in the busyness of life and forget this all too often.

Dougie and I connected and had many conversations – some very deep and others very light-hearted and funny. He had a way of telling stories that was fascinating to listen to. Such was the rapport between us that we got to a stage where we were open with each other about everything. The making of the documentary came up in the course of our conversation one day. We talked about how it would be very different to anything else on TV.

Following that conversation, Dougie contacted me and told me that he wouldn't mind participating in the programme. This was really difficult for him, but it was something he wanted to do.

In the beginning, he was coping with his illness and physically was doing well. There were days when he knew he would be able to talk on camera, and there were days when he just didn't have the energy. He was curious about everything that would happen after he passed, and I went through every detail with him. He wanted to see where he would be taken after death to be prepared for his funeral. We had many phone calls, and I hope that I was able to help him in some way when we talked. Still, though, it was a very difficult time for him and his family, as it is for any person going through terminal illness of any kind.

Dougie's final visit to Enniscrone was very poignant, but there was a great sense of peace around all of us that day. Dougie's last weeks were spent in a hospice. The staff there were remarkable, and it was a good reminder of how much exceptional support such places can provide.

Dougie had had very clear wishes about his funeral. We had strict instructions about what could or couldn't be filmed. One thing that was clear was that everyone who turned up to his funeral had great memories of him and wanted to give him and his family the respect they deserved.

Around the same time as Dougie's participation in the documentary, another family allowed us to film the wake of their dad. Anthony was a well-known man who had given lots of time to Irish culture and music. Gillian managed to film the wake in the funeral home in the most discreet way, while also being sensitive to people's wishes not to appear on camera. The cameras were turned off without any fuss if a person didn't want to be filmed as they paid their respects to the family of the deceased man.

There were other funerals where, in hindsight I wished I'd had the courage to ask the bereaved, as many of them praised the documentary afterwards and said that their relative would have loved to have their funeral documented and their life celebrated in this way.

Shannon Crematorium kindly allowed us to film their process of cremation while they explained what happens from start to finish. This was an area I knew people often wonder about, and the documentary was able to allay many of the false myths around cremation.

The trickiest part of filming was the embalming of the deceased. I was very conscious of the dignity of the deceased person and the need to maintain respect at all times. Gillian and her camera crew were very sensitive to this, working quietly and reverently in the mortuary. It was challenging for them to work in a mortuary, but they knew that their work was very important. This type of filming was different to anything they had previously done and was emotionally challenging at times. Many elements of the filming came with logistical and technical hurdles.

I trusted Gillian and her team to do a good job in crafting the documentary. I was confident that I had been able to
ensure, through the many conversations with her, that the
topic was going to be covered thoroughly and in a way that
was respectful and not sensational. I have to admit, though,
that even with this trust, I had a sick feeling on the day that
the documentary was aired in Ireland. I couldn't sleep the
night before, worried that it might offend someone or rake
up painful memories. That was something I would never
have wanted.

I was relieved when I saw the full documentary, which
was titled *The Funeral Director*. I have since received many
letters and emails from people in many different countries
thanking me for bringing comfort to them through the film.
They said that they found the way I had explained everything most helpful in understanding what goes on behind
the scenes once you say goodbye to a person, entrusting
them to the care of a funeral director and embalmer. Many
have talked about how it has helped them to cope with
death, especially when it was someone very close to them
who had passed away.

Many have also told me that it has helped them to
address their own mortality, and has led them to talk
about what they want to happen when they die. This is so
important, as none of us know when death will knock on
the door, so having these conversations proves very helpful
for a number of reasons. Discussions on topics like organ

donation, preferred funeral ceremony, place of burial or what is to be done with ashes if cremation is involved, all ease the huge burden on the bereaved. This was everything I had hoped for. I am so aware of how hard so many still find it to talk about death, but the documentary opened up conversations.

I am grateful to Gillian for the wonderful approach she took to the whole documentary. The edit must have been so difficult for her, with hundreds of hours of footage accumulated over a number of years.

In the end, Gillian had got it just right.

Looking Back . . .

I SOMETIMES THINK BACK to that young man who started helping Johnny with the funerals, all those years ago, at the back of the pub. Though I think on some level I knew that working with the bereaved was my calling from the off, I could never have envisaged the journeys I would go on or the wonderful people whom I would meet because of my profession. Not least because the job of a funeral director was not even considered to be a full-time career back then in Ireland. I have come a long way from that young man being taught how to line a coffin by Johnny, and what people want and need from a professional when someone they love dies has evolved too.

I really appreciated the help I got from others along the way, some simply pointing me in the right direction and others imparting their knowledge. This has inspired me to want to share my learning in the same way.

In 1990, after I opened my custom-built funeral home in Ballina, County Mayo, word quickly spread around the country in quite a unique way. In those days, the companies that sold coffin handles, side sheets, breast plates, habits, etc., to the funeral business had representatives travelling around the country. This was long before Facebook, and there were no trade journals or anything, so these very likeable people, whether they realised it or not, through going from business to business and sharing news, connected funeral directors around the country.

Unknown to me, shortly after it was finished and opened, my funeral home became a talking point among funeral directors around the country. Things like a foyer with a fireplace and a separate mortuary were new ideas to so many at the time in rural Ireland. Even just the idea of a funeral home was rare for rural areas and towns outside of the cities. As photos couldn't be emailed or shared on social media back then, they could only imagine what my building was like from the descriptions they heard. There was also a lot of talk connected with my recent return from studying mortuary science in the United States. So there was a double interest in me around the country, which I was unaware of until I began to get visits from funeral directors from every part of Ireland.

I was happy to see them and proudly gave guided tours of my premises as I explained all the different aspects of my modern funeral home and how it worked. I made some very loyal friends through these visits and I am very pleased to say that many of these good people are still true friends to this day. Many were fascinated by what I had achieved and were eager to learn more about embalming and new ways of funeral directing. I shared the plans of my funeral home with many. Some used them with very little change to develop their own funeral homes, while others adapted them to suit their own circumstances. Some might look on this as them exploiting me in some way, but I saw it as a great honour that what I had done was worthy of copying. I was willing to help other funeral directors improve the service they offered in their part of the country.

I realised that there was a great hunger for information on and insights into embalming. Those who had witnessed the results of different techniques in embalming were eager to learn more, plus there were funeral directors who were fascinated by the process, having never heard of it before. Just like when we'd had to call in Billy Doggert from Belfast to help us with the man in the church, they would have had their own difficult cases and were very keen to know more about a technique that would help them to avoid embarrassing and upsetting situations where things had gone terribly wrong with the deceased in their care. Information on the topic was not readily available in the British Isles at the time. It was fresh territory for many, and before the internet, and with very few books available on the topic, there weren't many other options available other than to do the correspondence course I had done and seek practical training with one of the few funeral directors that embalmed in one of the cities, or go abroad.

Some of the older funeral directors started bringing their sons to see me, wanting me to train them. There was a very strong tradition at the time of businesses being passed on to a son in the family to keep the family name. This practice changed over the years, and I am glad to say that women are now also highly respected in the funeral profession. Many of these young people came and stayed for a week or two, shadowing my work to learn more about the business. It would usually turn out that this wasn't long enough for them, and after they had gone, they would regularly contact me with queries, eager to learn more. In these days, many funeral directors still had a very limited knowledge of embalming, and the solution was to simply close the coffin if there was a problem. I remembered how hard it was to find information when I was a student, and I was happy to help on a voluntary basis. For some, 'eaten bread is soon forgotten' but many others often acknowledge my help, which had helped them get established on their career path. I am glad to say that many of these, in turn, have been willing to share their knowledge with the next generation of embalmers.

As time went by, I decided I needed to put some structure to what I was teaching all these students. Two large funeral directors in Cork and Dublin helped with this, with their qualified embalmers continuing the training process. I also brought on board qualified tutors in England with whom I worked closely, and they were willing to offer students placements in order to learn the practical side of embalming if they were willing to travel to the UK. Peter Ball and Malcolm Smith, officers on the national committee of the British Institute of Embalmers, were a huge help and a great inspiration to me.

Peter and Malcolm were also a huge support to me when it came to setting up our own Professional Embalmers' Association of Ireland. They could see that because Ireland has different funeral traditions to those of the UK, with a strong emphasis on the presentation of the deceased for the wake or a repose in a funeral home. Our embalmers have slightly different priorities, and it makes little sense to do everything through the professional body of another country. Helping to set up the organisation was very satisfying (although not without its difficulties at times, as is so often the case!), as it meant I was able to contribute to improving things across Ireland. The British Institute of Embalmers was a wonderful resource for me over the years, and I remain very thankful for all their work.

I established The Irish College of Funeral Directing and Embalming, the first of its kind in the country, which has been running for many years now. A large number of students have studied and qualified as embalmers through the college, and many have chosen to train and upskill in different areas of funeral directing and specific embalming techniques. Many guest speakers from abroad have given lectures in the centre over the years too.

In 2010, I lost a good friend and fellow funeral director, Tony Foley. Tony was something of a father figure to me, and it had already been agreed that I would take over his business, although Tony had intended to work alongside me for a while on a part-time basis. Sadly, it was never to be as he died following a short illness.

There was a complication in that Tony's funeral home had no embalming facilities, and it was at around this time that hospitals were stopping funeral directors from using their mortuaries due to more regulations being introduced and less space being available. So I found a premises and built a state-of-the-art facility out of town. I've since been asked by the council if, in the event of a disaster resulting in lots of fatalities in the area, they could use my mortuary, and I agreed.

I went on to develop a centre of excellence as part of the site, with lecture rooms where students can learn theory. I am delighted that we have very mixed groups of students from all backgrounds. There is also a very good gender balance – in fact, we've seen more women than men showing interest in the course in recent years. Many come to an open day to learn about the course to see if it is the calling for them. They find out about what is involved to hopefully equip them to make the decision as to whether it is something that they want to pursue. After all, it is more of a vocation than a job, and, on contemplation, some decide that they need to give the decision more thought. Others pursue the course with enthusiasm.

Some students come from a funeral business background while others are just drawn to it. Some begin the course eagerly, but at some point along the way decide that it is not the career path for them. Many of these seek out other ways of working with and helping the bereaved, as they have a genuine calling.

When choosing to do a course in funeral directing and embalming, it is important to do it for the right reason. It is work that involves commitment. If you want the quality of your work to be excellent, you must be prepared to prioritise it over other things. This is what makes it a difficult career in which to strike a good work/life balance. There are some close to me who might say that work has often won out in my life! I am fortunate that those same people also understand me, and ultimately I am forgiven, as they too value the importance of my work. Unfortunately, there are still people working in the profession whose work I think falls far short of the standard needed to show respect to the deceased and the bereaved. I can't do much about this, but it is a comfort to know that I have played my part in passing on what I have learned to those who are eager to learn.

I like helping people, and I find it very fulfilling helping students and colleagues alike. I could never have envisaged the places that this desire to teach others would bring me to, over the years. The first talks I gave were here in Ireland, when I shared my learning from America with my colleagues. As time went by, that extended to the UK, and I was sharing techniques that I had been taught in Chicago with British embalmers. We learned from each other, and I came to realise that we had the advantage of being able to work with the deceased within a day of death, whereas in the UK this was not the norm. In fact, it could be at least a week before an embalmer would be able to begin their work, which makes their job much more difficult.

I had also taken a keen interest in restorative work when I was in America. This involves reconstructing damaged tissue, when areas such as the face have been badly affected by an accident or serious illness. This was something that others were keen to learn about on this side of the Atlantic, as the most common practice at the time was just to close the coffin rather than trying to restore the appearance of the deceased so their relatives could see them to say goodbye.

Returning to the United States as a guest speaker of the New Jersey Funeral Directors' Association was a great honour for me. Over the years, I've found these sorts of events to be great places for sharing knowledge and comparing funeral cultures and traditions. The Irish traditions were of huge interest to the funeral directors at these conferences, who were fascinated with our way of looking after our dead. While America has promoted high standards and excellence, our way is different but highly respected. The funeral sector in the United States is strictly regulated and licensed, whereas neither the UK nor Ireland have a licensing system for embalmers or funeral directors. And yet we have a tradition of carrying out funerals with great dignity and respect, which was fascinating to some of my US counterparts. I guess our culture holds us firm to many of our beliefs and practices in relation to funerals.

I recall being invited to Lithuania by an embalmer who was keen to promote embalming there. I had never been to Lithuania, so the trip was exciting. I wasn't sure what equipment would be available to me when I got there, so I decided to bring the basics with me, including a basic pump.

They were really interested in learning how I embalmed. It was a joy to teach this group of people, as they were so enthusiastic and wanted to learn as much as possible. My basic pump was the first embalming machine that they had ever used. I believe it was placed in their embalming museum in Vilnius afterwards! The interest generated from this initial training session led to the formation of an embalmers' association in Lithuania, who subsequently joined the European Association of Embalmers. I know it was the initiation of a great interest in the subject, and I am proud to have been part of that process.

Learning about funeral traditions in other countries has been of great benefit to my colleagues and me. While there are commonalities across many of the European countries I have visited, it has also been interesting to learn how funeral directors in each jurisdiction have overcome problems with the deceased arising from circumstances unique to each area. For some, weather determines everything; for others, there are laws that they have to comply with that haven't necessarily always been made with the comfort of the bereaved at heart.

I believe that sometimes the best way of understanding what you are doing and the reasons for it is to be rigorously questioned about it by someone from outside of your own country, who does not necessarily see your ways as the 'norm'. It is in explaining to others the reasoning behind everything you do that you truly start to understand *why* you do things in a certain way, allowing you to develop a better understanding in the process. You start to really value what is your own, and see clearly the core values that need protecting as the whole funeral process evolves with modern society.

Travel has also enlightened me and helped me to learn, understand and respect different religious beliefs from around the world. Our country now has people from many different religious traditions, which is very different to back in the 1970s when Catholics and Protestants were the dominant faiths, with others existing mostly in small groups around the country. We as a country have embraced the rights of all to practise their belief systems here, in harmony with those around them. Likewise, different funeral traditions are now accepted and practised here, and, as a result, I have adapted my work to suit the needs of different beliefs.

But whatever the faith of the person who has been bereaved, or if they have none, what remains core to my work as a funeral director is supporting the individuals. Grief can affect rational thinking. It is therefore necessary for the funeral director to guide the bereaved through the period of a funeral, through the mixed emotions of mourners. As an independent person outside the core group involved in a funeral, I can empathise but still manage things in a rational and compassionate way. This skill transcends all belief systems.

EVEN IF THE family business had been something different, Aileen and I would still, I think, believe that it is vital to talk to children about death. Our daughters grew up knowing that death is a part of life itself. They were very aware of 'the sad people' from a very young age and, unsurprisingly, have great sensitivity to the loss experienced by those whom we meet every day in our work.

It's strange, but as parents, we never visualised our daughters in any particular career. We just wanted them to find their own strengths and make their way into suitable jobs that would make them happy in their lives. We most certainly never saw a need for them to follow the same career paths as us, and, if anything, always encouraged them to explore different things.

Mary, our eldest daughter, worked for a year in the funeral home before going to university in Galway to pursue a science degree, followed by a master's at Trinity College, Dublin. Bríd was fully focused on her musical career and pursued a degree and master's in music in Cork. Eithne used a skill she has learned in fusing glass to help the bereaved, incorporating ashes into the bespoke pieces, although she soon began to take a further interest in funeral directing and embalming too.

The three of them have all qualified as embalmers, showing great talent and empathy in their work. They are also fully trained funeral directors as well. It was interesting to see them develop, forging their own paths in life, and it was a bonus for me to see them find their calling in the funeral profession, with interest in different aspects of the work. They have all worked in the funeral home, carrying out duties from embalming to driving the hearse to supervising a repose.

They have an innate respect for the deceased, and also sense other connections with the deceased in a spiritual way. Most importantly, they are sensitive and have a deep understanding of the grief and loss experienced by the bereaved. They are very tuned in to the pain death brings, in many different ways.

I know that I would like to see them one day taking over the business that I have given my life to, as they each have their own individual contributions to make. And it's been a pleasure to see Mary's fiancé, Éanna Mulchrone, recently join us in the business, too. However, I know too that they need to make time for their other talents in music and the arts, as we all need a work/life balance.

What can be hard for me at this stage is to accept new concepts that they bring to the business. This is ironic, really, as they remind me of what I was like when I was their age, with dreams to fulfil and youthful ideas that are full of hope and tuned in to the needs of the younger generation. Their influence now keeps me on my toes.

Styles and fashions change, and in any job it's good keep up to speed with modern trends. However, you have to be cognisant of people wanting to keep with tradition, and the well-known rituals are often reassuring to those who have just lost someone close to them.

I am blessed to have a lovely staff working with me now, who maintain the dignity of the deceased and are sensitive to the needs of the bereaved.

We are a highly social species, and deep within us is a need to connect with others. This is very relevant at the time of a funeral. We need the support of others as we perform the rituals that have been built up over time to help us say goodbye to someone, so we invite others to come through the obituary notice. It is, in a way, our call for help, as well as our way to publicly declare our respect for the deceased and our deep sense of loss.

Funerals are so important to us here in Ireland, partly because we have such a strong sense of community, of the *meitheal.* We empathise and sympathise with the bereaved, feeling their pain, reminded of our own in the process. We support each other as much as possible. Of course, the Covid-19 pandemic that began in 2019, and the restrictions that were brought in to safeguard people, shattered this whole process. We could no longer gather as a community to say goodbye to the deceased and support the bereaved.

However, Irish people are resilient and creative, so instead of being miserable at home, unable to support people through their funeral process, something very powerful happened. It was very emotional for me to experience people coming out in solidarity, though socially distanced and outdoors. They lined the roads as a funeral procession crept slowly by, raising their hands in a farewell gesture to say goodbye to the deceased. There was such power in this action, and while a cruel virus had kept people apart in the days that led up to a death, both deceased and bereaved were surrounded by love and an overwhelming sense of community support.

People participated in funeral rituals from their own homes as everyone became more familiar with online social media platforms. Where restrictions permitted, many sat in cars outside of the church or building where the funeral was taking place, to be as present as they could in body and in spirit, just the other side of a wall.

However, it was still – as we all found – a very difficult time. Because our funeral rituals are such a big part of our culture, and such a vital part of the grieving process, many who were bereaved in this period suffered added heartbreak. The situation was made even sadder and quite frustrating by some of the recommendations made by the Irish Association of Funeral Directors to its members, recommending that anyone who had died with suspected Covid should be placed in two body bags in a closed coffin, and buried or cremated as soon as possible after they had died. The Professional Embalmers' Association of Ireland had reached out to them to share their knowledge about dealing with contagious diseases, but they were not taken up on the offer.

Throughout that time, the Professional Embalmers' Association of Ireland was taking guidance from the World Health Organization, the European Centre for Disease Prevention and Control and the Centers for Disease Control and Prevention in the US, none of whom recommended we cease embalming. The Irish government did not legislate in relation to care of the deceased, but instead kept a focus on limiting numbers of people that could gather in any one place at that time, including funerals. No law was ever made to say we could not embalm. In fact, the country's chief medical officer stated that the recommendations of the Irish Funeral Directors' Association were unnecessary.

However, most funeral directors throughout the country, whether they were members or not, still heeded the guidance of the Irish Association of Funeral Directors, which were published through national media. Things were so chaotic at the time that many thought this IAFD guidance was law. Sadly, the actions of the IAFD resulted in many people not being able to say goodbye to their loved ones, who may have died alone in hospital.

As a teacher and lecturer in the field of funeral directing and embalming, and, of course, as someone with a team of people working with me whom I am charged with keeping safe, I kept a close eye on the guidance issued and updated by the World Health Organization on how those working with those infected with a disease could best protect themselves from the threat of infection, and I knew that we could continue to embalm and allow families to say goodbye, as long as we followed the right precautions.

The precautions required were not new to me. For one, my time in Chicago coincided with the early stages of the AIDS epidemic, and the rules were clear and strict. We followed the guidelines, but we also respected the friends and relatives of those who had died having suffered from

AIDS prior to death. I learned how to hygienically treat the remains of an AIDS sufferer and enable their loved ones to be able to safely spend time with them. In my experience, the healthcare professionals who worked with AIDS sufferers were exceptional, and they led the way by treating their patients with kindness and compassion.

For many years, I have been called upon by hospitals to look after the remains of persons who have died from infectious diseases like AIDS, tuberculosis, hepatitis B and CJD, to name a few. Although Covid was a new disease, the principles were the same. We learned how it was transmitted, and we had all the information available to us to allow us to work safely and give the bereaved the closure they so desperately needed in this horrible time. I even offered free upskilling courses to other funeral directors if they did not feel they understood the correct practices well enough, though I was slightly disappointed by how few responded.

I spoke out publicly about this issue on many occasions, including on our national broadcaster RTÉ and numerous radio stations, as I felt passionately that it was totally unnecessary that people should be buried or cremated without their family's involvement and the necessary dignity. I was verbally abused by some, who would not heed the information coming from the scientific community and called me reckless.

The reality was that the deceased, who were not coughing or sneezing or moving, when hygienically treated with chemicals many times the strength of hand sanitiser, presented no risk to the living. The main danger was that if a living person with the virus touched the hands or forehead of the deceased, they could potentially leave the virus on the skin of the deceased, to be picked up by the next person to touch them. So we limited contact with the deceased to those closest among the bereaved and paid careful attention to social distancing.

While we hope to never have to go through a pandemic again in our lifetimes, we might, and it is very important to evaluate what happened and learn from how it was approached. We need to note what could have been done differently. I believe that in researching this, the bereaved should be consulted, as their varied experiences may well lead to us finding solutions to the problems that arose. I hate to think of how many are still coming to terms with the extra pain of not being able to see and say goodbye to their loved ones back in 2020.

I WOULD LOVE for us to be comfortable talking openly about death. The younger generations are leading the way in encouraging all of us to be more open about our emotions, and I hope it follows that conversations about death will also become the norm.

For one, it is important to talk to others if you have particular wishes for your funeral. This makes the burden of arranging a funeral so much easier for the bereaved. They won't have to worry, trying to second-guess your wishes, and they can add their own elements to the funeral process to help them to cope and begin to work through their grief. The funeral marks the beginning of the grieving process for those we leave behind, as well as being a celebration of someone's life and a way of honouring them.

There will be memories of us left in the minds and hearts of others. Some good, some bad, some we were intentionally party to, others that we might not even be aware of. I am reminded of this every day in my working life.

Being in constant contact with people who are grieving has shown me how grief can shut down our normal ways of coping with happiness and sadness in our lives. Until it happens to us, we have no way of predicting how our brains will react. I have seen some of the most organised people I know fall apart following the loss of a person very close to them. I have also seen people of great faith become completely disconnected from their religion for a period of time. For some, life feels meaningless for a while, and everything that had been a priority or a joy before the loss of a loved one becomes trivial.

There can be nothing more annoying than someone reminding you that 'time heals', when, deep down, the idea of healing seems impossible, because you are trying to come to terms with the fact that someone you connected to and whose company you enjoyed above any other has gone. It breaks my heart when I talk to the bereaved in the months after a loss. When the hustle and conversations of a funeral are finally over and a great silence befalls the kitchen, that is often when the blow strikes hardest. That is the time when we need to go with the flow. That is the time to allow others to connect with us. We need each other to survive. Friends who give us space and understand as we grieve, but who also give us little nudges to continue to live are invaluable. The more we allow them in, the more little glimpses of hope we get.

In the conversations that I have with people about their death, they all say that they would want people to learn to enjoy life after they are gone. None of us would wish our relatives to embark on a life of mourning and tears after our death, would we? Of course, we don't want to be forgotten either. Children are very inspiring in this light. They teach us to hope and they don't forget the important things. They also believe and have great faith.

Whatever their faith, I encourage people who have suffered such a loss to connect with the natural world, as through it, we can often find hope. An impromptu sighting of a bird bopping along beside you, or watching beautiful plants grow, can open up our minds and hearts again, to help us process what is happening to us.

I have learned that a connection with nature is very important to keeping a balance in our lives. I am privileged to live in a rural area surrounded by the beauty of nature. I encourage others to take advantage of our natural amenities. There is nothing better than a walk on a beach, or in a forest, or sometimes simply down the road, to help us cope with the stresses of life.

Most of all, keep searching for help, be it through counselling, therapy, clairvoyants, clergy or simply a good friend, until you find a way of coping that really works for you. Some find solace in dedicating themselves to a certain cause, inspired by the loss they have experienced. The very act of helping others, while sharing their own experience, has helped some to survive horrific tragedy in their lives.

Never give up searching for a way that helps you to keep going.

We all arrived on this planet alone, and we will leave this planet alone, regardless of what we have done in this life. There is no point in being the richest person in the cemetery or crematorium. We will all leave all our worldly goods behind us one day.

I hope this book has brought you on a journey with me, that it has helped you to cope with death in whatever way it has affected you. I trust you have learned from it and that you can use that learning to help others.

My life among the dead has been a very unique one. It has been very difficult at times, as you can imagine. Being the leader for the bereaved isn't an easy task. Making difficult decisions requires courage.

It is a path that I have needed to follow. It has been decidedly different, but it has been the right path for me.

Two paths diverged in a wood, and I—
took the one less travelled by,
and that has made all the difference.

– Robert Frost, 'The Road Not Taken'

Acknowledgements

None of us can predict death. We can plan to a certain degree, but until it comes knocking at our door, we have no idea how we will be affected by it.

My life has been intertwined with death and the uncertainty of tomorrow. I have encountered many different circumstances where people have faced death and bereavement in their lives. There is no 'easy way' when it comes to death. It is painful in so many regards. A funeral is emotional and difficult to get through, even for the closest of families and friends. Helping the bereaved to navigate this journey is very fulfilling, but not without its challenges. A life among the dead takes its toll not just on me, but also on those closest to me, who have supported and understood my sorrow.

In my career, I have always prioritised education. There is no point in being set to help when death occurs, without having any idea how you will manage the situation and look after the deceased. Being truly ready to cope with as many situations as possible requires ongoing education.

My hunger for learning and sharing knowledge has brought me many friendships along the way from all over the world. Some have been like ships in the night, and others have been constantly there for me. These people have all enriched my life and work.

I have given many the opportunity to explore their calling to the vocation of caring for our dead. It is not a career for everyone, and there are many challenges and sacrifices to be made in its pursuit. Many of these people have gone on to pursue a career in death care while others have found different paths.

I am lucky to have been surrounded by teams of good people who have worked with me over the years. Sadly, some have since passed, and I am reminded of them throughout my daily work. I have a really good staff, who are kind, caring, efficient and very professional. This is so important when we work in a profession that affects each of us in different ways. Some days are very difficult, but the camaraderie behind the scenes helps get us through. It's not all doom and gloom, we also have good times together. I am thankful and privileged to have these people working with me, who give so much of themselves to their work.

I have been blessed to have encountered many special people who have given me hope and encouragement on my mission to help the dead and the bereaved. I thank each and every one of you. There are too many people to acknowledge individually, however there are a few who have had a profound effect on me and my work.

One such person was the late Val O'Connor in Cork. He was a huge inspiration to me and I am forever grateful for his support and friendship in my life.

To Martin and Eileen Hallinan, who made a home away from home for me in Youghal, when I worked and studied in Cork.

Thanks to Lesley Simpson, who led me to the path of education in death care, that began with Henry and Billy Doggert.

To Joan and Bruno at Worsham College, who took me under their wings when I was so far away from home.

To Mary Joyce Gleason and her family, and to Maureen O'Looney and the vibrant Irish community in Chicago, who made me feel at home when I was so far away from my friends and family in Ireland.

To the late Virginia 'Ginny' Lucania of The Montclair-Lucania Funeral Home in Chicago. Thank you for your knowledge and deep sense of care for the deceased that had a profound effect on me. To this day, I still remember your instruction and attention to detail.

Thanks to my friends and colleagues in the British Institute of Embalming. Back in the days when there weren't many embalmers in Ireland, this organisation gave us opportunities to meet up and talk as professionals. I particularly want to thank Malcolm Smith and Peter Ball, who were always supportive and championed educational events, as well as encouraging us to set up our own educational courses and independent organisations.

Thanks to Joe McNamara and all my friends and colleagues in the Professional Embalmers' Association of Ireland. Their friendship and support is always valued. Through this organisation, I have been fortunate enough to meet and work with many other professionals throughout the world.

To Martina Burns, for her dedication, support and friendship since she first came to work in the funeral home in 2002.

Thanks to Gillian Marsh at Marsh TV for creating *The Funeral Director* documentary. This was a difficult topic, but her approach was always sensitive, with a strong quest for accuracy and truth. She and her team teased through the many aspects of death care and managed to give the public insights into a topic that is so difficult for many. Years of work went into the documentary. Hundreds of letters are testimony to the fact that it has brought solace and comfort to so many as they cope with grief.

To Yvonne Jacob, Liz Marvin and all the team at Headline Publishing Group and Hachette Books Ireland for helping me through the process of writing this book. Thanks in particular to Yvonne. Your gentle nudges and encouragement were what helped me get this book over the line. Thank you for keeping me on track from start to finish.

To my lovely daughters Mary, Bríd and Eithne. You have grown up in a world dictated by funerals. It hasn't been easy for you, as I have had to juggle family life with death care and sometimes miss out on family occasions. You have grown up with a strong sense of empathy and understanding. It is an honour to me that you have all explored career paths in death care and it fills me with pride to be able to work with you.

To my wife, love and best friend Aileen who has been there for me over the years. Thank you for your continued support and for your help in writing this book, keeping me on course throughout. Thanks for your patience over the years. Your empathy has always been underpinned by the sudden loss of your dear mam, Bridie, in 1989. I appreciate the understanding you have always shown when others were in need of my care at a time of great sorrow.

Finally, thanks to everyone who has been good to me in my life. No matter how small the acts of kindness, you can never underestimate the difference they can make to others.